What Kind Of Church Do You Want?

What Kind Of Church Do You Want?
Prepared For Newburgh Theological Seminary

A Dissertation
By
Robert E. Crout

Edited
By
Wesley G. Vaughn

To Newburgh Theological Seminary
In Partial Fulfillment of the Requirement For
The Degree of Doctor of Theology
April 2, 2012

Newburgh Press Newburgh, Indiana

Newburgh Press, Newburgh, Indiana
Copyright © 2012 Robert E. Crout

ISBN: 978-0-9909250-9-5

All rights reserved. No portion of this book may be reproduced, stored in a retrieval system, or transmitted in any form or by any other means - electronic, mechanical, photocopy, recording or any other except for brief quotations in printed reviews and school or ministry related studies, without the prior permission of the author.

All Scripture quotations, unless otherwise indicated, are from the King James Version, 1611.

This book and all other books by Newburgh Press are available worldwide. Books may be ordered through your local bookstore or on the Internet through book dealers such as Amazon.com, BarnesandNoble.com and wherever books are sold.

Bibliography in alphabetical order.

Printed in the United States of America

ABSTRACT

The intention of this dissertation is to provide the individual and families with information on various forms of church government and practices, what to expect when looking for a church, and based upon personal expectations, the various methods used in determining what kind of church that would best provide the individual and families with solutions to problems normally discovered in attempts to find the best church for them. The Bible clearly shows us that the "church" is not a structure or a building but rather a body of believers. Since the church is very important to believers, one of the most important decisions that one can make is choosing a place to worship.

TABLE OF CONTENTS

ABSTRACT VI
TABLE OF CONTENTS. VIII
INTRODUCTION TO THE STUDY X
CHAPTER ONE 1
    CHURCH GOVERNMENT 1
    EPISCOPAL FORM 2
    PRESBYTERIAN FORM 7
    CONGREGATIONAL FORM 10
    THE BIBLICAL PATTERN 14
CHAPTER TWO   CHURCH DOCTRINE. 17
    THE CHURCH 17
    THE WORK OF THE CHURCH 21
    MAJOR CHURCH DOCTRINE 22
    DOCTRINE OF THE APOSTLES 24
    DOCTRINE DEFINED 27
    SOUND DOCTRINE. 27
    CHURCH DOCTRINE 28
    NICENE CREED. 29
    MOST CHRISTIANS BELIEVE 30
    SPECIFIC CHURCH DOCTRINE 33
        BAPTIST DOCTRINE 33
        METHODIST DOCTRINE. 37
        PRESBYTERIAN DOCTRINE 39
        LUTHERAN DOCTRINE 42
        PENTECOSTAL DOCTRINE 44
        OTHER DOCTRINE 46
        BAPTISM 47
CHAPTER THREE   MAJOR ISSUES. 51
    CALVINISM 51
    ARMINIANISM 53
    INSPIRATION AND INERRANCY 56

CHAPTER FOUR   THE SCRIPTURES 59
   INTENTIONAL ERROR 61
   GOD'S PEOPLE DESTROYED? 64
   OLD AND NEW 65
CHAPTER FIVE   WHY GO TO CHURCH? 67
   CONCERNING SPIRITUAL GIFTS 69
CHAPTER SIX   LEAVING A CHURCH 73
   ANOTHER VIEW 76
   CONTEMPORARY (CHRISTIAN) MUSIC
   DEFINED 78
   THE CHOICES 81
   WHAT KIND OF CHURCH DO YOU NEED? . . 81
   WHAT KIND OF CHURCH DOES JESUS
   WANT? (JOHN 17) 83
   WHAT KIND OF GOD DO YOU WANT? 86
   WOULD JESUS ATTEND YOUR CHURCH? . . 87
CHAPTER SEVEN   CHOOSING A CHURCH 91
   CONCLUSION 104

BIBLIOGRAPHY 107

APPENDIX I   CHICAGO STATEMENT ON
BIBLICAL INERRANCY 111
   PREFACE 111
   SHORT STATEMENT 113
   ARTICLES OF AFFIRMATION AND DENIAL 114

APPENDIX II. 121
   THE CHICAGO STATEMENTS ON
   BIBLICAL HERMENEUTICS 121
   ARTICLES OF AFFIRMATION AND DENIAL 122

Introduction To The Study

A concern of Christians is the proper selection of a church that not only adequately meets the family and individual needs, but one that can utilize the experience and knowledge of the potential member. A quote by C.S. Lewis in the preface of his book *Mere Christianity* relates a truth not generally thought of when searching for a church or already in a church that one may not appear to be satisfied with: "In plain language, the question should never be: 'Do I like that kind of service?' But, are these doctrines true: is holiness here? Does my conscience move me toward this? Is my reluctance to knock at this door due to my pride, or mere taste, or my personal dislike of this particular door keeper?" (Lewis 1972).

This project is intended to answer two central questions: To what extent do we concern ourselves with the selection of a church in a Christian environment or to remain in a church that we are currently in? The other question is related to the church itself: In view of the first question, will your church be functioning tomorrow? The essential problem is that many families and individuals look for a church by just attending a service or two and make selections without understanding problems that may arise. Making selections too quickly may result in beginning the process again. Many times there are problems within the church that cannot be within view of the public, difficulties that the church may be experiencing internally causing decline.

This work is about public worship with the objective to explain what happens on a typical day of worship as it relates to different forms. The primary objective is to make the reader aware of various forms of worship that can be expected in various denominations, such as Methodist, Baptist, Presbyterian, etc., and various forms within denominations.

Questions must be answered as to the basic understanding of denominations such as service structure, type of worship, and what form of church government is practiced. Do I enjoy freedom of worship in an informal atmosphere or would I be more comfortable with liturgy, a formal atmosphere? The objective is to be aware of structure that would conflict with style not in conformity with one's tradition and to arouse curiosity about unfamiliar forms.

Consideration of doctrinal issues is important, especially as it concerns those who are well educated or informed on doctrinal matters. Although not very often asked for, a copy of the church's statement of faith would be important. A very important element of worship is related to doctrinal questions as to the individual's acceptance of Arminian or Calvinistic understanding. Before making a decision, one should understand essential doctrines such as the Trinity, Incarnation, Redemption, the Resurrection of Christ and others. "—they continued steadfastly in the apostles' doctrine and fellowship, in the breaking of bread, and in prayers" (Acts 2:42). Even though other studies have included information related to the above doctrinal issues, the objective of this study is to relate doctrine to the issue of discovering a church one could adapt to.

The type of worship is one of the most important factors that should be carefully considered. Some churches have traditional music using hymns while others are much less formal, using contemporary music with bands and "worship teams", (a much overused phrase, sometimes without adequate meaning). Consideration should be given to preference in services that may provide a mixture of hymns and contemporary music. The important question should be answered as to your comfort zone in such a mix. Much research has been done on types of music in churches, but most of these studies relate to the view of the investigator and the effect of personal opinions. This study will be confined to the different types of worship related to music and arguments of Biblical application.

The most important of all criteria for final determination of your selection of a church is to ask the question, "Does this church believe that the Bible is the inerrant, inspired Word of God?" Inerrancy and inspiration will be considered in detail, especially in view of current trends that appear to disregard Scripture which is contrary to individual way of thinking, or to attempt to alter the original meaning of Scripture to suit individual desires.

Motivation for this research began when there appeared to be families changing churches for many different reasons, triggering a requirement of a response that was problematic. Inquiring as to reasons of changes did not result in any one problem but multiple motives. Adults and youth had dissimilar reasons and the various surveys provided broad but unsatisfactory results. Youth are leaving churches and even religion itself for many reasons. Many of these problems have been approached by surveys generally in forms that ask specific questions. This study will take a different approach with the general idea of attempting to create solutions to certain problems by concentrating on major reasons for individuals and families desire to change churches.

The overall theoretical approach to this study will be to study denominational structure, doctrine, and types of worship of Christian organizations. It is important for the individuals and families searching for a new church or providing guidance and leadership to the church they are currently worshiping in, to be knowledgeable about the church conditions. To facilitate understanding of the question, "What kind of church do you want?" it is necessary to understand denominational structure. This includes forms of church government, various Christian denominations and general practices of those denominations, variations of Scripture, music, and choosing a church suitable for various individuals and families.

CHAPTER ONE
CHURCH GOVERNMENT

Church government is that branch of ecclesiology that addresses the organizational structure and hierarchy of the church. There are three basic types of structure that have developed in the various denominations; the Episcopal, the Presbyterian, and the Congregational. One may be concerned at this point that there are certainly more than three, but keep in mind that these are types of government that are found in various Christian organizations, not denominations.

"It appears likely that there was no normative pattern of church government in the apostolic age and that the organizational structure of the church is no essential element in the theology of the church" (Ladd 1993). As we will see in the following dialog, all three basic types of structure maintain Biblical evidence. Even though they differ in form, none creates a pattern that differs basically in theology, meaning the practice based primarily upon the text of Scripture. In this, we define theology as the study of God and of God's relation to the world.

"It is not as much as hinted in the New Testament that the church would ever need—or indeed should ever want or tolerate—any other leadership than that of the eldership group" (J. A. Motyer 2000). Motyer was obviously referring to the Presbyterian form of government. As we will see, both the episcopal form and the congregational form are also worthy of study. Studying all forms will be edifying and provide a better understanding of church government in general. There are actually no pure forms of any of the three types of church government. Most churches use mixed forms, so when using the term "episcopal," for example, the basic discussion is about those churches in which the various episcopal forms are primary.

EPISCOPAL FORM

The most highly structured form of church government is the Episcopal form with authority residing in the bishop. This form, most highly developed, has been the polity of the Roman Catholic Church from as early as Ignatius of Antioch, all the way to the time of the Reformation. The Church of England explains that the bishop of a diocese is the party responsible for the diocese. The diocesan bishop is the chief pastor of all that are within his diocese, both laity and clergy. They have particular responsibility for apostolic teaching and doctrinal orthodoxy as well as responsibility for worship, the right of conducting, ordering, controlling, and authorizing all services. The authority of the

Episcopal form of government resides in the bishop, suggested by Titus 1:5 and 7: "For this cause left I thee in Crete, that thou shouldest set in order the things that are wanting, and ordain elders in every city, as I had appointed thee—for a bishop must be blameless, as the steward of God; not given to wine, no striker, not given to filthy lucre."

Advocates derive their position from the Old Testament as well as church history. Episcopalians, Catholics, Eastern Orthodox, and Anglicans take this hermeneutical approach from an Old Testament interpretation of Moses' organizational method as per Jethoro's suggestions (see Exodus 11 and 12). Some have appealed to the Melchizedek model of pastoral and legal hierarchy for the church as well. The Exodus 18 interpretation leads to not only a hierarchy but a clear division between clergy and laity. Many ignore this division. These adherents take the Greek word episcopos, meaning overseer, to be the foundational core for their biblical hermeneutic. They also point to Mark 6 to argue that since Jesus organized the fish eaters into groups of fifties and hundreds, He must have intended for the church to establish this pattern. So they place a bishop over a diocese, an archbishop over bishops, and have synods to serve as advisory councils (Burch 2010).

This has been traditionally the setup of Episcopalian, Catholic, and Methodist churches, and those who have a hierarchy with one person at the head. That person may be called a pope, bishop, elder, etc., but all with the essential head referred to as bishop. The Greek word "episkopo" means "those who rule", of which the word "bishop" is derived.

The bishop has considerable power, including ordination of ministers and priests. The Roman Catholic Church teaches that when the pope speaks in his official capacity in matters of faith and practice, he is said to be infallible. The office of the Bishop in the New Testament was a ruling office. "Let the elders that rule well be counted worthy, especially those who labour in the word and doctrine" (1 Timothy 5:17). In this verse, the Bishop (or Elder) is recognized as both ruling and preaching. Peter provided several guidelines for elders of the churches: "The elders which are among you I exhort, who am also an elder, and a witness of the sufferings of Christ, and also a partaker of the glory that shall be revealed: Feed the flock of God which is among you, taking oversight thereof, not by constraint, but willingly; not for filthy lucre, but of the ready mind" (1 Pet. 5:1-2).

A second part of an elder's job includes "taking oversight." Peter is careful to emphasize that the pastor does not have dictatorial rights: "Neither as being lords over God's heritage, but being ensamples to the flock" (1 Pet. 5:3). These elders were challenged to lead the congregation for the right reasons. Therefore, the indications are, that the pastor who preaches should also rule, but they are to rule well, not to dictate or control. This exercise of leadership rule is by example.

One of the chief strengths of the episcopal form of church government is that it provides an example in the model of a leader for others to follow. The apostle Paul was a gifted leader who recognized his opportunity to influence several generations of leaders. He told Timothy, "And the things that thou hast heard of me among many witnesses, the same commit thou to faithful men, who shall be able to teach others also" (2 Tim. 2:2) (Towns 1971).

Examples of specific Episcopal forms of government include:
- The Roman Catholic Church
- The Eastern Orthodox Church
- The Oriental Orthodox churches
- The Assyrian Church of the East
- The Churches of the Anglican Communion
- The Nazarene Churches
- Numerous smaller Catholic churches
- Certain national churches of the Lutheran confession
- The African Methodist Episcopal Church
- The United Methodist Church

Some Lutheran churches practice the Presbyterian or Congregational form of church government. Many Methodist churches maintain the form and function of the episcopal, but modified (Swatos 2006). Regardless what the "governance is called, if final authority rests in one person, then that church has an episcopal form of government in reality. This is true of many independent churches with a single strong leader. A church with a senior pastor who holds final authority would also be an example of episcopal polity" (Knox 2010).

Some organizations and churches have modified the episcopal form, such as The Foursquare Church, by not granting unlimited authority to any individual thereby providing freedom for certain leadership roles. People are appointed to positions and then allowed to make honest mistakes as they grow. At the same time, they do not give unlimited authority to anyone.

The Foursquare Church is also blended with elements of both Presbyterian and congregational structures developing a hybrid of all three.

Candidates for ordination in the Foursquare Church must follow strict forms, and have at least a Master of Divinity (M.Div.) with comprehensive examinations.

PRESBYTERIAN FORM

Presbyterianism was founded by John Knox in the early sixteenth century A.D. to share government among the plurality of leaders. Multiple lay elders that are elected by the congregation to represent them, is reflected in the United States Government as well. Opponents of Presbyterianism argue that lay elders, usually called ruling elders, do not at all fit the Biblical description. Presbyterian ministers are usually teaching elders while the ruling is done on a corporate level by a session or council. The Greek word, presbyteros, meaning older, is the basis for this pattern.

Presbyterians cite two sources of authority for their elder-led polity, namely the Pauline narratives and the constitution of the Presbyterian Church. They refer to Paul's pattern for establishing the practice in Gentile congregations. "And when they had ordained them elders in every church, and had prayed with fasting they commended them to the Lord on whom they believed" (Acts 14:23). As to the Jewish implementation, reference is made to Acts 15:6, "And the Apostles and the elders came together for to consider this matter" (Burch 2010).

The Presbyterian form places primary authority in a particular office as well but with less emphasis on the individual office. Typically, the authority that the church believes Christ gave to us is said to reside at the local elder level, indicating that as the highest authority, after Christ. Even though the Greek word for bishop and elder seem to be used interchangeably in places, final authority is the difference between the episcopal and the Presbyterian government. Final authority rests in one person in the episcopal form, while the final authority rests in a group in the Presbyterian form. Acts 15:6 provides an example of the Presbyterian form of management when "the apostles and elders came together for to consider this matter".

This form is practiced by the Presbyterian and other churches who allow a presbytery, or council of elected trustees, deacons, or stewards, to make major decisions for the body. Authority is placed on the office but with less emphasis on the individual elders or deacons which are typically elected by the congregation on a periodic basis (usually a term of about three years). Those who are elected to office are to serve their terms as the spiritual and theological leaders of the congregation. There is sometimes a distinction between the elders, especially non-clergy who take part in pastoral care, and deacons geared toward the care of members and families. The Office of Elder, a position in the Jewish synagogue, is the key officer in the Presbyterian structure. Elders in the New Testament were prominent men. The term elder is interchangeable with the term bishop. Those appointed or elected were of high caliber and qualified to rule the church. In the Old Testament, they were in a governing capacity (Erickson 1998).

Those who fill the office of elder must meet rigid spiritual requirements. The requirements are set forth clearly in the New Testament (1 Timothy 3) and the Book of Church Order, the governmental standard of the church. The teaching elder "should possess a competency of human learning and be blameless in life, sound in faith, and apt to teach…" Those who fill the office of ruling elder should also be "be blameless in life and sound in faith: they should be men of wisdom and discretion: and by the holiness of their walk and conversation should be examples to the flock."

Teaching elders are ordained by the presbytery after they, as candidates under the care of presbytery, have followed a prescribed course of study in college or theological seminary. A presbytery may ordain a candidate only when he has received a call to a definite work. Usually the call is from a congregation to become its pastor, although a candidate may be ordained as a teacher or evangelist (Rev. E.C. Scott 1972).

Presbyterian government is historically a confessional tradition, adhering to the Westminster Confession of Faith. Scriptural uniformity can easily be seen in the "apostolic" Presbyterian general assembly at Jerusalem (cf. Acts 15). In fact, this general assembly "delivered decrees" that were binding on all individual churches that were a part of the one visible church which adhered to apostolic doctrine. The Greek word used for "decrees" in Acts 16:4, is "dogmata." Compare this with the word "decree" used in Luke 2:1. The same word as used in Luke 2:1 is referring to the decree of Caesar Augustus regarding his call for an empire wide census. This was not a suggestion given by Caesar, nor was it just advice that could be ignored without penalty—it was law! In the same way, the decree sent down by the general assembly that took place in Acts 15 was to be held as law for the church. These decrees were carried out from Jerusalem to the churches in the cities of Asia Minor, as well as Antioch, indicating that the scope of the synod's authority extended not only over the church at Antioch, which made the original request, but over all the churches (Presbyterian and Independency 1995).

CONGREGATIONAL FORM

The third form is the Congregational government implied in Acts 15:22, "– It pleased the apostles and elders with the whole church to send chosen men of their own company to Antioch with Paul and Barnabas". This time the apostles and elders asked the opinion of the whole church. This form "stresses the role of the individual Christian and makes the local congregation scheme: autonomy and democracy. By autonomy we mean the local congregation is independent and self-governing" (Erickson 1998).

At the heart of Congregationalism is the belief that the local congregations are to govern their own affairs. This stands in contrast to both Episcopacy and Presbyterianism. Within the scope of Congregationalism there are a variety of ways in which the relationship between the local church leaders is construed. In this regard, the spectrum reaches all the way from a full-fledged democratic model to elder rule with various forms of church leadership and congregational rule or participation in between these two extremes (Kosteberger n.d.).

The principal of autonomy means that each local church is self- governing, calls its own pastor and determines its own budget. Property is independently purchased and owned. It may seek advice from other churches but is not bound to follow that advice, and no actions require outside approval (Erickson 1998).

Jesus and Paul assigned the responsibility for discipline to the group as a whole. Jesus discussed the treatment of a brother who had sinned (Matt. 18:15). Paul instructed the congregation as a whole (I Cor. 5).

"It is the intention under congregational polity that the congregations govern itself under the lordship of Jesus Christ (Christocracy) and with the leadership of the Holy Spirit (pneumatophoria) with no superior or governing ecclesiastical bodies (autonomy) and with every member having a voice in its affairs and its decisions (democracy)" (James Leo Garrett 2001).

There are some congregations that choose not to associate on a sustained basis with other congregations and some who freely choose to affiliate and support denominational bodies for educational, benevolent, or other purposes. Passages in the New Testament, such as Matt.18:15-20, could refer to a local congregation. Verses 15-17 relate to offences that are under the authority of a local congregation. In Acts 6:3, most modern and pre-modern commentators hold that the Seven were chosen by the entire congregation. The words, "they were worshipping," in Acts 13:2 "ISV" are taken by most to refer to the congregation (James Leo Garrett, An Affirmation of Congregational Polity 2005).

Henry Ainsworth, a separatist, very clearly spelled out the essential features of congregational polity. The same was true of the Separatists' document *The True Confession 1596*, and also of John Robinson, who "stood," as Timothy George has said, "at the convergence of" Separatism and Independency (George 1982).

Within at least thirty-five different Protestant denominational bodies in the United States other than the Baptist conventions, it is said that congregational polity is being practiced. Scripture gives evidence that congregational government was practiced in the New

Testament. When personal offences occurred the local church was to solve the issue, not the pastor (Matt. 18:15-17) and to discipline sinning members (1 Cor. 5:1-5). When the pastor sins, he is also rebuked by the congregation (1 Tim. 5:20).

When the church in Jerusalem needed men to assist the apostles and take care of the widows, the multitude of believers elected them (Acts 6:1-7). The congregation commissioned Barnabas and Saul as missionaries (Acts 13:1-3) and when they returned from their mission, they reported to the church (Acts 14:27). The church sent men to Jerusalem to solve doctrinal issues (Acts 15:1-3). Many other references occur that will confirm congregational organization.

In summary, Christ takes both the right and the power to judge teaching from the bishops, scholars, and councils and gives them to everyone and to all Christians equally when he says in John 10, "My sheep hear my voice" (v.27). Again, "And a stranger they will not follow, but will flee from him for they know not the voice of strangers" (v. 5). All that ever came before me are thieves and robbers. but the sheep did not hear them.

Have you seen clearly who has the right to judge doctrine: Bishops, popes, scholars, and everyone else have the power to teach, but it is the sheep who are to judge whether they teach the voice (i.e. the words) of Christ or the voice of strangers? (Luther 1906).

THE BIBLICAL PATTERN

The three prominent forms of church government all appeal to the Scriptures as well as church tradition for support of their respective positions. Since the Bible is not silent on the subject, key elements in the Bible are germane.

• There is no distinction between "elders" and "bishops." "For this cause left I thee in Crete that thou shouldest set in order the things that are wanting, and ordain elders in every city, as I had appointed thee: if any be blameless, the husband of one wife, having faithful children not accused of riot or unruly, for a bishop must be blameless, as a steward of God; not self-willed, not soon angry, not given to wine, no striker, not given to filthy lucre" (Titus 1:5-7). "And from Miletus he sent to Ephesus, and called the elders of the church…Take heed therefore unto yourselves, and to all the flock, over which the Holy Ghost hath made you overseers, to feed the church of God"(Acts 20:17, 28).

• Each congregation and center of leadership is to have plenty of elders, not one-man rule. "And when they had ordained them elders in every church, and had prayed with fasting, they commended them to the Lord, on whom they believed (Acts 14:23). "And from Miletus he sent to Ephesus and called the elders of the church" (Acts 20:17).

- These elders have oversight of the church. "Take heed therefore unto yourselves, and to all the flock, over which the Holy host hath made you overseers, to feed the church of God; which He hath purchased with His own blood" (Acts 20:28) and are thus responsible to rule the congregation. "For if a man know not how to rule his own house, how shall he take care of the church of God? (1 Tim. 3:5). They judge among the brothers (cf. 1 Cor. 6:5) and in contrast to all the members, they do the rebuking "Them that sin rebuke before all, that others also may fear" (1 Tim. 5:20). Christ calls them to use the "keys of the kingdom" to bind and loose: "Whatsoever ye shall loose on earth shall be loosed in heaven (Matt. 16:19; 18:18). These keys are the beginning of the preaching of the gospel, administering of the sacraments (1Cor. 11:23-34) and the exercise of discipline (1 Cor. 5:1-5).
- The elders are assisted in their ministry by "deacons" who give attention to the ministry of mercy (Acts 6:1-6; cf. I Tim. 4:14).
- The office bearers in the church are nominated and elected by the members of the congregation: "And the saying pleased the whole multitude: and they chose Stephen, a man full of faith and of the Holy Ghost, and Philip, and Prochorus, and Nicanor, and Timon, and Parmenas, and Nicolas a proselyte of Antioch: Whom they set before the apostles: and when they had prayed,

they laid their hands on them" (Acts 6:5-6). Notice that it was the congregation who nominated the deacons and it was the examination and confirmation and ordination by the present board of elders that placed them into service (Acts 6:6).

• Members of the church have the right to appeal disputed matters in the congregation to their elders for resolution (Acts 15) (Bahnsen 1991).

CHAPTER TWO
CHURCH DOCTRINE

THE CHURCH

The word 'church' in the New Testament is translated from the Greek word 'ekklesia' (ek-Klay-see-ah), which comes from two words; 'ek' meaning 'out' and 'kaleo' meaning to call. An 'ekklesia' or 'calling out' was not just an assembly. The words agora and paneguris as well as heort, koinon, thiasos, sunagogge and sunago can all mean an assembly. The word 'ekklesia' was a political term, not a religious term. Jesus was the King and the Bible used the term 'ekklesia' for a good reason. In classical Greek 'ekklesia' meant "an assembly of citizens summoned by the crier, the legislative assembly (R. Scott n.d.).

In our English Bible, the word "ekklesia" is translated in most places, "church". The word "ekklesia" is mentioned in the Bible one hundred fifteen times. It is translated in English "church" one hundred thirteen times and two times translated "assembly".

Israel is described as a church in that it was a nation called out from the other nations to be servants of God. "This is He that was in the church in the wilderness with the angel which spake to him in the Mount Sinai, and with our fathers: who received the lively oracles to give unto us" (Acts 7:38). When the Old Testament was translated into Greek the word "congregation" (of Israel) was rendered "ekklesia" or "church." Israel then, was the congregation or church of Jehovah. After His rejection by the Jewish church, Christ predicted the founding of a new Congregation or church, a Divine institution that should continue His work on earth (Matt. 16:18). This is the church of Christ, which came into existence on the day of the Pentecost (Pearlman 1937).

The creation of the New Testament church, then, was by Jesus Christ about 2000 years ago. He was recognized as the King by the existing world government when Pontius Pilot had Jesus nailed to the cross. 3000 were baptized into that church at Pentecost in one day. Acts 2:41 indicates that they were added to the church, indicating that the church was in existence at that time.

"When Jesus came into the coasts of Caesarea Philippi, He asked His disciples, saying 'Whom do men say that I the Son of man am?' And they said, some say that thou art John the Baptist: some say, Elias; and others Jeremias, or one of the prophets. He saith unto them, 'But whom say ye that I am?' And Simon Peter answered and said, Thou art the Christ, the Son of the living God. And Jesus answered and said unto him, 'Blessed art thou, Simon Barjona: for flesh and blood hath not revealed it unto thee, but my Father which is in heaven.

And I say unto thee, that thou art Peter, and upon this rock, I will build my church; and the gates of hell shall not prevail against it' (Matt. 16:13-18).

There is a need for clarification of these verses which have been misquoted many times, even in some later versions of Bible. The word "Peter" is transliterated from the Greek word "petros" in the "Textus Receptus" (the received text). The Greek word "petros" means "stone or small piece of a rock". Some translate "Peter" as "the rock", changing the meaning. Jesus Christ is the rock, the corner stone, on which the church was built. Notice that this was Christ's church and it will be built upon the solid rock, Christ Jesus, the builder and maker. Jesus said, "Thou art Peter (Petros, a piece of a rock) and have the name of a stone, but upon this rock (Petra, the Solid Rock; the Foundation Stone) pointing to himself, "I will build my church". "For other foundation can no man lay that is laid, which is Christ Jesus" (1 Cor. 3:11). "Wherefore also it contained in the Scripture, Behold, I lay in Sion a chief cornerstone, elect, precious: and he that believeth on Him shall not be confounded" (1 Pet. 2:6). Christ is both the founder and the foundation.

The purpose of the church is clear from Scripture. "Then Jesus came and spake unto them saying, 'All power is given unto me in heaven and earth. Go ye therefore, and teach all nations, baptizing them in the name of the Father, and of the Son, and of the Holy

Ghost: Teaching them to observe all things whatsoever I have commanded you: and lo, I am with you always, even unto the end of the world.'" (Matt. 28:18-20). This should be the main purpose in any church. Some churches take a primary role of care of believers, focusing inward on building itself up. The focus of many churches is self-help programs, finances, popular books, etc., omitting the primary purpose of the church.

Another purpose of the church is that believers might be as one. "Our Lord especially prayed that all believers might be as one body, under one head animated by one soul by their union with Christ and the Father in Him, through the Holy Spirit dwelling in them. The more they dispute about the lesser things, the more they throw doubts upon Christianity. Let us endeavor to keep the unity of the Spirit in the bond of peace, praying that all believers may be more and more united in one mind and one judgment. Thus shall we then convince the world of the truth and excellence of our religion and more sweet communion with God and His saints" (Matthew Henry's Commentary on the Whole Bible, John 17:20-23).

When looking for a church, or determining the value of remaining in a church, the above understanding is important. What does the church teach? Are they following the real purpose of the church?

THE WORK OF THE CHURCH

- **To Preach Salvation:** It is the work of the church to preach the gospel to every creature and to expound the plan of salvation as taught in the Scriptures. Christ has made salvation possible by providing it; the church must make it actual by proclaiming it.
- **To Provide a Means of Worship:** Israel possessed a divinely appointed system of worship by which they approached God in all the needs and crises of life. The church likewise must be a house of prayer of all people where God is honored in worship, prayer, and testimony.
- **To Provide Religious Fellowship:** Man is a social being; he craves fellowship and an exchange of friendship with those who share the same interest.
- **To Hold up the Moral Standard:** The church is "the light of the world," to banish moral ignorance; to preserve it from moral corruption. The church must teach men how to live as well as how to die. It must hold forth God's plan for the regulation of all spheres of life and activity. Against the downward trends of society it must lift a warning voice; at all danger points it must plant a beacon light (Pearlman 1937).

MAJOR CHURCH DOCTRINE

It should be a major factor before choosing a church to determine the doctrine of that church. The word "doctrine" literally means "teaching" or "instruction" and is further understood as the fundamental truths of the Bible arranged in systematic form. "If ye know these things, happy are ye if ye do them" (John 13:17). "Study to show thyself approved unto God, a workman that needeth not to be ashamed, rightly dividing the word of truth" (2 Tim. 2:15). There is a difference between a doctrine and a dogma. A Biblical doctrine is God's revelation of a truth as found in the Scriptures; a dogma is man's statement of that truth as set forth in a creed (Pearlman 1937).

Pearlman says in his introduction to his book, "There is a tendency in some quarters not only to minimize the value of doctrine but to dismiss it as outgrown and useless. However, as long as men think about the problems of existence they will feel the need of an authoritative and systematically arranged answer to these problems"(Pearlman 1937).

"It is striking that every time false doctrines (doctrines of devils and strange doctrines) are mentioned which do not correspond with the teaching of the Holy Scriptures, the word 'doctrine' is written in the plural – 'doctrines.' Where the 'doctrine' of the Holy Scriptures is spoken of, the word 'doctrine' is always written in the singular with clear instructions to 'teach no other doctrine' (1 Tim. 1:3 & 10, cf 1 Tim. 4:1 & 6 and 1 Tim. 6:3); this principle is also found throughout the other epistles of the New Testament. This means that the Bible only knows one doctrine" (Leith 2012).

Paul told Timothy to stay in Ephesus in order to advise some that they teach no other doctrine, and not to give in to fables and endless genealogies: "Also of your own selves men shall arise, speaking perverse things, to draw away disciples after them (Acts 20:30). By adding to the Word of God, false doctrines result in organization of cultic religions. Timothy was advised to be certain that no strange doctrines would be taught.

"What characterizes the sound doctrine? 1 Tim. 1:5 says, 'Now the end of the commandment is charity out of a good heart, and of a good conscience, and of faith unfeigned' (1 Tim. 1:5)." Paul is referring to law and doctrine, inferring the difference between good sound doctrine and false doctrine; pure love, pure heart, and pure faith (Leith 2012).

It is important to understand what a church teaches before becoming a part of an unknown. Sound doctrine is of supreme significance when choosing a church. Choosing a church depends on your theology (school of thought) if you know what that is. "…prove what is that good, and acceptable, and perfect will of God" (Rom. 12:2b).

DOCTRINE OF THE APOSTLES

"And they continued steadfastly in the apostles' doctrine and fellowship, and in breaking of bread, and in prayers" (Acts 2:42). The doctrine of the apostles is the teachings of the apostles. Jesus equated doctrine with teachings in Matthew 16:6 when He told His disciples to be aware of the leaven of the Pharisees and the Sadducees, the religious teachers of their day. Even though the disciples thought He was talking about food at first, He was talking about false doctrine (false teachings). Jesus called these teachings hypocrisy (Luke 12:1), meaning to act in a way that you are not in reality.

The Apostles' doctrine was what the apostles taught by the authority of Christ, through the inspiration of the Holy Spirit, as recorded in the New Testament. The Apostles established doctrines and practices of the church that God had established. Their doctrine included almost everything in the New Testament.

It must be understood that "Whosoever transgresseth and abideth not in the doctrine of Christ, hath not God. He that abideth in the doctrine of Christ, he hath both the Father and the Son. If there come any unto you, and bring not this doctrine, receive him not in your house, neither bid him God speed: For he that biddeth him God speed is a partaker of his evil deeds" (2 John 9-11).

The intent of the reformers was to restore the Apostles'

doctrine. Realizing that the church was deviating from biblical teachings, they developed what was known as the "five cries of reformation":

- **Sola scriptura** – Scripture alone explains the means of salvation. The Bible contains all knowledge necessary for salvation and holiness. All authorities are subjective to the written word of God. Scripture alone is authoritative for faith and practice of the Christian. Tradition cannot be superior to Scripture since the Bible is God-breathed, inerrant, and authoritative.
- **Sola fide** – The doctrine of justification by faith alone, one of the key points that separate true biblical gospel from false gospels. It also separates Protestant belief and Roman Catholic belief as well as most other religions and teachings.
- **Sola gratia** – Salvation by grace alone is the hallmark of Protestant theology. If anything of human effort is added to the grace of God then salvation is not by grace alone. Jesus said "My grace is sufficient" for you.
- **Solo Christo** – We are saved through the person of Christ alone, not Christ plus sacraments, or works, but Christ alone. "Then Peter, filled with the Holy Ghost, said unto them, ye rulers of the people, and elders of Israel, if we this day be examined of the good deed done to the impotent man, by what

means he is made whole, be it known unto you and to all people of Israel, that by the name of Jesus Christ of Nazareth, whom ye crucified, and whom God raised from the dead, even by him doth stand here before you whole. This is the stone which was set at naught of you builders which is become the head of the corner. Neither is there salvation in any other: for there is none other name under heaven given among men, whereby we must be saved" (Acts 4:8-12). John the Baptist said, "Behold the Lamb of God who takes away the sin of the world" (John 1:29).

- **Soli Deo Gloria** – Salvation is to the glory of God alone. Whether therefore you eat, or drink, or whatever ye do, do all to the glory of God (1 Cor. 10:31).

The original meaning of *Sola scriptura* was to describe the means of salvation. The apostle's doctrine plays an important role in the faith of believers everywhere and is not to be taken frivolously. If there are more than fifty references in Scripture made to "doctrine," the "doctrine of Christ", the "Apostles doctrine", "wholesome doctrine" and "sound doctrine", should there be any doubt as to the importance of teaching doctrine?

DOCTRINE DEFINED

A study of the word "doctrine" in the New Testament will reveal four primary areas of concentration presenting a progression of truth for consideration of the apostles' doctrine. In the Book of Acts the word "doctrine" is found four times; the "apostles' doctrine" in Acts 2:42, "your doctrine" in Acts 5:28; the "doctrine of the Lord" in Acts 13:12; and the "new doctrine" in 17:19.

SOUND DOCTRINE

In the Pastoral Epistles, we find the word, "sound doctrine" or "good doctrine" mentioned numerous times. "As I besought thee to abide still at Ephesus, when I went to Macedonia, that thou mightiest charge some that they teach no other doctrine" 1 Tim. 1:3). The Defenders Bible comments that "doctrine" (teaching) is often downgraded today in the church in favor of an emphasis on love. Nevertheless, sound doctrine must come first. Christian love is a natural product of sound doctrine (1 Tim. 1:5) (Morris 1995).

1Timothy 1:10-11 describes what is contrary to "sound doctrine," but "good doctrine" continues in 1 Tim. 4:6 "…good minister of Jesus Christ, nourished up in words of faith…" The apostles' doctrine then must have a healthy and positive impact on our manner of living.

Notice many action verbs associated with the word "doctrine"; give attendance, take heed, labor in, make known, preach, rebuke, exhort, convince, speak thou, show a pattern, adorn...the doctrine. Notice in Mark 1:21-22 that "they were astonished at His doctrine; for He taught as one that had authority...". Jesus had spoken a "new doctrine" (vs. 27), taking authority to cast out demons. In Mark 11:17-18, the scribes and chief priests were amazed at His "doctrine".

Doctrine cannot be compromised, as we read in 2 John 9-11. The doctrine of Christ was the doctrine of the apostles. The doctrine of Christ then must be all the teachings of Christ, everything He said and did, covering all Scripture and all His purposes.

CHURCH DOCTRINE

Church doctrine can be defined as a written body of teachings of a religious group generally accepted by that group. Understanding church doctrine as it applies to various church bodies is of great importance during the process of searching for a church.

As outlined earlier, there are essential doctrines that the Christian must believe. Even though not stated exactly in Scripture, some doctrine is taught in most all Protestant churches. Most of the doctrine of the church is derived from the Nicene Creed (AD 325).

This creed is the only creed accepted by all three major branches of Christianity: Orthodox, Roman Catholic, and Protestant.

NICENE CREED

I believe in one God, the Father Almighty Maker of Heaven and Earth, and of all things seen and unseen, and in one Lord Jesus Christ, the only-begotten Son of God, Begotten of the Father before all ages: God of God, Light of Light, true God of true God; begotten, not made, being of one substance with the Father; by whom all things were made.

Who for us all our salvation, came down from Heaven, and was made incarnate by the Holy Spirit of the virgin Mary, and was made man; He was crucified also for us under Pontius Pilate; He suffered and was buried; and the third day He rose again, in accordance with the Scriptures; and ascended in Heaven, and sits at the right hand of the Father; And He shall come again, with glory, to judge the living and the dead; whose kingdom shall have no end.

And I believe in the Holy Spirit, the Lord and Giver of Life; who proceeds from the Father; who with the Father and the Son together is worshipped and glorified; who spoke by the prophets.

And I believe in one holy universal and apostolic

Church. I acknowledge one baptism for the remission of sins; and I look for the resurrection of the dead, and the life of the world to come. Amen.

MOST CHRISTIANS BELIEVE

There are principles of doctrines that most all Christians believe.

I. Rule of Faith and Practice
   a. The Divine Inspiration and Authority of the Canonical Scriptures in matters of faith and morals. (Against Rationalism)
II. Theology
   a. The Unity of the Divine Essence. (Against Atheism, Dualism, Polytheism)
   b. The Trinity of the Divine Persons. Father, Son, and Holy Ghost, the Maker, Redeemer, and Sanctifier. (Against Arianism, Socinianism, Unitarianism)
   c. The Divine Perfections. Omnipotence, omnipresence, omniscience, wisdom, holiness, justice, love, and mercy.
   d. Creation of the world by the will of God out of nothing for His glory and the happiness of His creatures. (Against Materialism, Pantheism, and Atheism.)
   e. Government of the world by Divine Providence

III. Anthropology
   a. Original innocence. Man made in the image of God, with reason and freedom, pure and holy; yet needing probation, and liable to fall.
   b. Fall: sin and death. Natural depravity and guilt; necessity and possibility of salvation. (Against Pelagianism and Manichaeism.)
   c. Redemption of Christ
IV. Christology
   a. The incarnation of the eternal Logos, or second Person in the Holy Trinity.
   b. The Divine-human constitution of the Person of Christ
   c. The life of Christ. His superhuman conception; His sinless perfection; His crucifixion, death, and burial; resurrection and ascension; sitting at the right hand of God; return to judgment.
   d. Christ our Prophet, Priest, and King forever.
   e. The mediatorial work of Christ, or the atonement. "He died for our sins, and rose for our justification".
V. Pneumatology
   a. The Divine personality of the Holy Spirit
   b. His eternal Procession (from the Father, and His historic mission by the Father and the Son.
   c. His divine work of regeneration and sanctification.

VI. Soteriology
   a. Eternal predestination or election of believers to salvation.
   b. Call by the Gospel
   c. Regeneration and conversion. Necessity of repentance and faith.
   d. Justification and sanctification. Forgiveness of sins and necessity of a holy life.
   e. Glorification of believers.
VII. Ecclesiology and Sacramentology
   a. Devine origin and constitution of the catholic (universal) church of Christ
   b. The essential attributes of the Church universal. They are Unity, catholicity, holiness, and indestructibility of the Church; Church militant and Church triumphant.
   c. The ministry of the gospel
   d. The preaching of the gospel
   e. Sacraments: visible signs, seals, and means of grace
   f. Baptism for (because of) the remission of sins
   g. The Lords Supper for the commemoration of the atoning death of Christ.
VIII. Eschatology
   a. Death in consequence of sin
   b. Immortality of the soul
   c. The final coming of Christ

d. General resurrection
   e. Judgment of the world by our Lord Jesus Christ
   f. Heaven and Hell; the eternal blessedness of saints, and the eternal punishment of the wicked.
   g. God all in all (I Corinthians 15:28) (Schaff 2009).

SPECIFIC CHURCH DOCTRINE

There are doctrines that are specific to various denominations that in general, comply with the doctrine that all Christians believe. However, in view of the purpose of this dissertation, there is an importance in indicating what certain denominations believe. Baptists believe that they have fundamental doctrines of faith that defines them.

BAPTIST DOCTRINE

The Bible is God's Word. It was written by men whom God inspired and is His revealing of Himself to man. It is perfect because it has God for its author, salvation as its primary message, and truth without error. The Biblical truth is that "All Scripture is given by inspiration of God, and is profitable for doctrine, for reproof, for correction, for instruction in righteousness: That the man of God may be perfect, thoroughly furnished unto all good works" (2 Tim. 3:16-17).

There is one and only one living and true God. He is an intelligent, spiritual, and personal Being who is the Creator, Redeemer, Preserver, and Ruler of the universe. God is infinite in holiness and perfect in every way. "That men may know that thou, whose name alone is Jehovah, art the most high over all the earth" (Psa. 83:18). "Go ye therefore and teach all nations, baptizing them in the name of the Father, and of the Son, and of the Holy Ghost" (Matt. 28:19). God as Father reigns supreme with providential care over His universe, His creatures, and the stream of human history according to the purposes of His divine grace. "Grace be to you and peace from God the Father, and from our Lord Jesus Christ" (Gal 1:3).

Christ is the eternal Son of God. In His incarnation as Jesus Christ He was conceived of the Holy Spirit and born of the virgin Mary. Jesus is perfectly revealed in Scripture and did the will of God by taking upon Himself human nature with its demands and necessities. In doing so, He identified Himself completely with mankind, yet without sin. "But these are written, that ye might believe that Jesus is the Christ, the Son of God; and that believing ye might have life through His name" (John 20:31).

God the Holy Spirit is the fully divine Spirit of God. He inspired those men of old whom He chose to write the Word of God. Through illumination, He enables men to understand God's truth as revealed in His Scriptures. "If ye then, being evil, know how to give good gifts to your children: how much more shall your heavenly Father give the Holy Spirit to them that ask Him?" (Luke 11:13).

Man is the special creation of God who made us in His own image. He created us male and female as the crowning work of His creation. In the beginning man was innocent of sin and was endowed by His creator with freedom of choice. By His free choice man sinned against God and brought sin into the human race. "Wherefore, as by one man sin entered into the world, and death by sin; so death passed upon all men, for that all have sinned" (Rom. 5:12).

Salvation involves the redemption of the whole man, and is offered freely to all who accept Jesus Christ as Lord and Savior. It is Jesus who, by His own blood, obtained eternal redemption for all who believed. "For he saith, I have heard thee in a time accepted, and in the day of salvation have I succored thee: behold, now is the accepted time; behold, now is the day of salvation" (2 Cor. 6:2).

All truly born-again believers endure to the end. Those whom God has accepted in Christ and sanctified by His Spirit will never fall away from the state of grace nor can they lose God's gift of eternal life. They shall persevere to the end. "And I give them eternal life; and they shall never perish, neither shall any (man) pluck them out of my hand" (John 10:28).

A New Testament church of the Lord Jesus Christ is an independent local congregation of baptized believers, associated by covenant in the faith and fellowship of the Gospel. The church observes the two ordinances of Christ, which are the Lord's Supper and Believers Baptism. It is governed by His laws while exercising the gifts, rights, and privileges invested in those who identify with it by His Word, seeking to extend the gospel to the ends of the earth, "Take heed therefore unto yourselves, and to all the flock, over which the Holy Ghost hath made you overseers, to feed the church of God, which he hath purchased with his own blood" (Acts 20:28).

God, in His own time and in His own way, will bring the world to its appropriate conclusion. According to His Word, Jesus Christ will return personally and visibly in glory to the earth. The dead will be raised, and Christ will judge all men in righteousness according to God's will. "For the Lord Himself shall descend from heaven with a shout, with the voice of the archangel, and with the trump of God; and the dead in Christ shall rise first: then we which are alive (and) remain shall be caught up together with them in the clouds, to meet the Lord in the air: and so shall we ever be with the Lord. Wherefore comfort one another with these words" (I Thess. 4:16-18).

METHODIST DOCTRINE

The Methodist church traces its roots back to 1739 in England as a result of the teachings of John Wesley. Wesley's three basic precepts that began the Methodist tradition consisted of: (1) Shun evil and avoid partaking in wicked deeds at all costs, (2) Perform kind acts as much as possible, and (3) Abide by the edicts of God the Almighty Father. Methodist doctrine is more simply outlined than some other denominations. Wesley believed in the Bible as the Word of God, full inspiration and inerrancy, and that God revealed Himself in the Bible. In his Journal, volume 6, page 117, he writes, "... Nay, if there be any mistakes in the Bible there may as well be a thousand, If there be one falsehood in that book it did not come from the God of truth."

Methodist doctrine is summarized as:
- God is all-knowing, possesses infinite love and goodness, is all powerful, and the creator of all things.
- God has always existed and will always continue to exist.
- God is three persons in one, the Father, the Son (Jesus Christ) and the Holy Spirit.
- God is the master of all creation and humans are meant to live in a holy covenant with him. Humans have broken this covenant by their sins, and can only

be forgiven if they truly have faith in the love and saving grace of Jesus Christ.
- Jesus was God on earth (conceived of a virgin), in the form of a man who was crucified for the sins of all people, and who was physically resurrected to bring the hope of eternal life.
- The grace of God is seen by people through the work of the Holy Spirit in their lives and in their world.
- Close adherence to the teachings of Scripture is essential to the faith because Scripture is the Word of God.
- Christians are part of a universal church and must work with all Christians to spread the love of God.
- Baptism is a sacrament or ceremony in which a person is anointed with water to symbolize being brought into the community of faith.
- Communion is a sacrament in which the participants eat bread and drink juice to show that they continue to take part in Christ's redeeming resurrection by symbolically taking part in His body (the bread) and His blood (the juice).
- Wesley taught his followers that Baptism and Communion are not only sacraments, but also sacrifices to God.
- People can only be saved through faith in Jesus Christ, not by other acts of redemption such as good deeds.

PRESBYTERIAN DOCTRINE

The Presbyterian movement traces its roots to Scotland with the 1707 "Acts of Union" which created the United Kingdom of Great Britain. The Presbyterian denominations in Scotland hold to the theology of Calvin. Presbyterian doctrine in general appears to be consistent in most of the churches even though there are differences in various branches.

Many of the Presbyterian beliefs are similar to other churches but defined somewhat differently.

As a system of doctrine, all Presbyterian beliefs are determined by a basic thought about God: that He is sovereign in all things. He governs His creation, His creatures and all their actions. Who God is provides the key to reality, not who man is. What God does provides the key to human experience, not what man does. What God works provides the key to salvation, not what man works. Everything that happens takes place according to the will of God.

As the result of Adam's sin all men are sinners; that sin is a stain upon us from our birth so that if left to the natural inclinations of our wills our lives would inevitably turn toward evil. The doctrine of total depravity also suggests man's helplessness. Human beings are not only sinful, they are also helplessly sinful.

God so loved us that while we were dead in trespasses

and sins that He sent forth His only begotten Son to redeem us. The Lord Jesus Christ, pre-existent with the Father, by Whom He created the worlds, came to earth by being born of the virgin Mary. He, the Eternal Son, took upon Himself our nature, lived a sinless life as a man and died on the cross in a sacrifice which somehow paid the price of our redemption from sin.

In keeping with the doctrine of Sovereignty, under which God is seen to determine all things, Presbyterians believe that the knowledge of Christ and the acceptance of Christ, which leads to Salvation, also come from God. We are saved by faith alone and this faith itself is a gift of God. Our personal redemption is not due to any goodness of our own for we have none; neither is it earned by our good works for sinners cannot accumulate "credit" leading to redemption.

Because Salvation is clearly not given to every man (although we know not why), Presbyterians therefore believe in Reprobation, or the eternally lost condition of those not elect.

The Election of God calls men to redemption in Jesus Christ so it calls them to newness of life in Jesus Christ. The Holy Spirit not only makes a child of sin to become a child of God, He also leads the new believer into a new way of life which is in conformity to the will of God, into holiness of life and sanctification.

Presbyterians believe in the Holy, catholic church; that

is, in the universal unity of Christ's body in time and eternity. As a vine and its branches comprise a single whole, so Christ and all those in whatever place or age derive their life from Him comprise a single Body, the Church universal. This church is not to be identified with any denomination or body on earth for it exists wherever a true child of God may be found.

Baptism and the Lord's Supper are the two sacraments that Presbyterians believe in, instituted by Christ Himself. They do not believe that the blessing is inherently present in the sacraments, but that they are rather signs and seals of the blessing they represent. As the Holy Spirit does not dwell in the pages of a Book, yet He warms our hearts by means of the message of that Book. The Lord's Supper not only shows forth the Lord's death until He shall return, but is a sacrament in which He is truly though spiritually present and truly though spiritually received.

Baptism is a sacrament which signifies and seals God's covenant promise to be a Father to His own and to their children. It visibly represents the way this promise is carried out in the coming of the Holy Spirit upon the life of those in whom the promise is fulfilled. Presbyterians believe in the return of Jesus Christ "to judge men and angels at the end of the world." Until He comes, the souls of those who die in Him depart to be with Him "where they behold the face of God in light and glory, waiting for the full redemption of their bodies." At the last day, the dead shall be resurrected and the living shall be changed, Christ's elect "unto honor…and everlasting life," but the reprobates "unto dishonor…and punishment with everlasting destruction from the presence of the Lord and from the glory of His power."

LUTHERAN DOCTRINE

Lutherans' beliefs and practices are similar to those of other churches in many ways but they trace their core beliefs and practices back to the principles of Martin Luther, the German monk known as the "Father of the Reformation." Luther's basic departures from the Roman Catholic doctrine were based on the following beliefs:

- Baptism – Although Luther retained the belief that Baptism was necessary for spiritual regeneration, no specific form was stipulated. Today Lutherans practice both infant baptism and baptism of believing adults.
- Individual Access to God – Luther believed that each individual has the right to reach God through Scripture with responsibility to God alone. It is not necessary for a priest to mediate.
- The Lord's Supper – Luther also retained the sacrament of the Lord's Supper, but the doctrine of transubstantiation was rejected.

- Sacraments – Luther believed the sacraments were valid only as aids to faith (initiating and feeding faith), thus giving grace to those who participate in them.
- Salvation by Grace through faith – Luther maintained that salvation comes by Grace through faith alone, not by works and sacraments.
- Salvation for All – Luther believed that salvation is available to all humans through the redeeming work of Christ.
- Scripture – Luther believed the Scriptures contained the one and necessary guide to truth.

Worship – As a matter of worship, Luther chose to retain altars and vestments and prepare an order of liturgical service, but with the understanding that no church was bound to follow any set order. As a result, there is today, no uniform liturgy belonging to all branches of the Lutheran body. However, an important place is given to preaching and congregational singing.

The above listing of beliefs and practices contains those of what are commonly referred to as the four "mainline denominations." To be further broken down, the list would be much larger and not rational to list. There are other churches such as Pentecostal, non-denominational, (meaning no part of a larger denomination), and inter-denominational, (bringing together of a range of other denominations), all with various practices and beliefs.

PENTECOSTAL DOCTRINE

Pentecostalism is a renewal of genuine Christianity that places emphasis on the new birth of an individual, and on a direct personal relationship with God through the baptism of the Holy Spirit. The baptism of the Holy Spirit will direct the one baptized with the twelve fruits of the Spirit (Holiness) and the nine Gifts (Power) of the Holy Spirit (Galatians 5:22 and 1 Corinthians 12:7-11: See also John 1:12-13).

"During the early revivals of 1900-1929, Charles Parham (1873-1929), an independent holiness evangelist who believed strongly in divine healing, was an important figure in the emergence of Pentecostalism as a distinctive Christian movement. In 1900, he started a school near Topeka, Kansas, which he named Bethel Bible School" (Wikipedia). In 1906, the only black student of Parham, William J. Seymour was not allowed to attend class among his fellow white students for the manifestations of the Holy Spirit; but while sitting outside, he received the plenitude of the Holy Spirit. After the Bible School experience, Seymour, baptized a Catholic, traveled to Los Angeles to hold a revival. When the church that he was invited to rejected his message, he looked for an alternative, found an abandoned building, placed planks of wood on nail crates for seating and began a revival that lasted for three years. It has been stated that the reason for the revival is that modern classical Christianity was missing the power and authority of the Holy Spirit. "The first Pentecostal converts were mainly from the Holiness movement and adhered to a Wesleyan understanding of sanctification as a definite, instantaneous experience and second work of grace. Problems with this view arose when large members of converts entered the movement from non-Wesleyan backgrounds, especially from Baptist churches. In 1910, William Durham of Chicago first articulated the Finished Work, a doctrine which located sanctification at the moment of salvation and held that after conversion the Christian would progressively grow in grace in a lifelong process (Synan, Pentecostalism: Varieties and Contributions 1987).

In 1914, a group of 300 predominately white Pentecostal ministers and laymen from all regions of the United States gathered in Hot Springs, Arkansas, to create a new, national Pentecostal fellowship— the General Council of the Assemblies of God.

The Pentecostal doctrine is in agreement with Methodism with the additions of:

- Water Baptism is only by immersion *(see Baptism page 47)*
- Baptism with the Holy Spirit as promised in Acts 1:4-8. (cannot be earned but received as a gift) at salvation, born of the Holy Spirit; At Pentecost, filled with the Holy Spirit.

- Gifts of the Spirit in 1 Corinthians 12:7-11 are all active gifts, "…given to every man severally as He will" (verse 11).

OTHER DOCTRINE

Other doctrine is clearly taught in Scripture, and essential doctrine is also clear and they can be summarized:
- The Trinity: God is three in one and one in three who is the maker of all creation.
- Incarnation: God sent His only begotten Son into the world to provide a way of Salvation. He was conceived in the womb of a virgin begotten by the Holy Spirit.
- Redemption: Jesus took upon Himself all the sin of mankind and died on the cross so that man can be united with Him.
- Atonement: Through Christ's death we are made one with Him.
- Resurrection: After Christ's death, he was placed in a tomb (grave) where he was triumphant over death and rose up on the third day.
- Ascension: After His resurrection our Lord ascended to His Father where He sits on the right hand of the throne making intercession for those who believe in Him.

- Sin: Through one man, sin entered into the world and as a result, all men are sinners (See Romans 5:12-21).
- Justification: Our only justification and righteousness is through Jesus Christ
- Death: Eternal death is separation of the body and the soul
- Judgment: At the second coming of Christ, every man shall give an account of himself before God and shall go into everlasting life or everlasting punishment. That sentence is irrevocable.

BAPTISM

There are doctrinal differences among various denominations, but the above listed ones are most important. What is practiced in various churches may be different in many cases, depending upon denominational beliefs. One of the most prominent differences is in the doctrine and mode of baptism. All believe that baptism is biblical but the question is: "What is the purpose and what is the mode?" Baptists, along with other denominations such as the Pentecostal, believe that the only method acceptable is immersion. Others believe in all methods including "sprinkling", "pouring", and "dipping", although Scripture is weak. Some who see water baptism only from a denominational and traditional perspective feel that those who insist on a certain form or mode are legalistic. Others believe that immersion is the mode that is more conformable to the New Testament pattern.

It is interesting that in previous generations, many church theologians accepted immersion as the only way:

- Martin Luther, the protestant reformer: "In the primitive church, baptism was a total immersion, or burial, as it were."
- John Calvin, Presbyterian theologian: "Baptize signified to immerse, and it is certain that immersion was the practice of the ancient church."
- Archbishop Cramer, martyred in 1556: "By baptism we die with Christ, and are buried, as it were."
- John Wesley, founder of Methodism: "Buried with Him alluding to baptism by immersion, according to the custom of the first church."
- Dr. Chalmers, first Moderator of the Free Church of Scotland: "Baptism is immersion."
- Dr. Pain, Congregationalist and Professor of Ecclesiastical History: "Immersion was the baptism of the Christian church for thirteen centuries."
- Dean Stanley, Episcopalian: "In the Apostolic age, those who came to baptism came in full age, and of their own choice. Those who were baptized were immersed."
- Bishop Bossuet, Roman Catholic theologian: "For

thirteen hundred years baptism was administered by immersion." (Mumford 1975)

According to the *World Book Encyclopedia*, we find that "At first all baptism was by complete immersion" (vol. 1, p. 651). The *Catholic Encyclopedia* states "In the early centuries, all were baptized by immersion in streams, pools, and baptisteries" (Vol. 2, p. 263).

Immersion was not convenient after the Catholic Church instituted infant baptism, thus the mode was changed to sprinkling. (See Encyclopedia Britannica, 11th ed., col. 3, pp.36566).

Another primary question indicated in church doctrines is, "What does baptism do?" It is generally considered to symbolize our death, burial, and resurrection with Christ. Some denominations teach that water baptism is necessary for salvation, claiming Luke 3:3 as reference. Some commentaries, such as Williams, include "baptism for a change of mind." Beck adds, "Repent and be baptized to have your sins forgiven." The primary reason for baptism in any instance is justified in Scripture.

CHAPTER THREE
MAJOR ISSUES

CALVINISM

Calvinism, originating with John Calvin, French theologian and pastor during the Protestant Reformation, teaches that God in His plan has chosen that some shall believe and thus receive the offer of eternal life. God foreknows what will happen because He has decided what will happen. This is true with respect to all other human decisions and actions as well. God is not dependent on what humans decide.

Most Calvinists believe that the purpose of Christ's coming was not to make possible the salvation of all humans, but to render certain the salvation of the elect. There are several elements in their argument.

There are Scripture references that teach that Christ's death was for His people. The angel promised Joseph in Matthew 1:21, "And she shall bring forth a Son, and thou shalt call His name Jesus: for He shall save His people from their sins." There are many other statements by Jesus regarding His sheep as in John 15:13, "Greater love hath no man than this that a man lay down his life for his friends" (Erickson 1998).

Another line of argument relating to Christ's

intercessory work is from R. B. Kuiper, who argues that John 17:9 deliberately limits to the elect the focus of Christ's high priestly prayer, "I pray for them: I pray not for the world, but for them which thou didst send me." Since Christ prayed exclusively for those whom the Father had given Him, it follows that they are the only ones for whom he died" (Kuiper 1959).

Martin Luther also wrestled with the subject of predestination. In connection with Romans 8:28, Luther points to God's absolute sovereignty with respect to humans in the Old Testament, particularly His election of Isaac and rejection of Ishmael, and His election of Jacob and rejection of Esau (see Rom. 9:6-18) (Erickson 1998).

Contrary to the verses in Romans 8:28 and 29 and 1 Peter 1:2, Henry Morris states that "The 'foreknowledge' of God involves more than just knowing ahead of time the choice that a given person will make, for 'known unto God' are all His works from the (foundation) of the world (Acts 15:18), and He 'worketh all things after the council of His will' (Ephesians 1:11). Those whom He foreknew He then created as 'the vessels of mercy, which He had afore prepared unto glory' (Romans 9:23). This in no way inhibits anyone who wants to be saved from coming to Christ, for He has invited all to 'come unto me' (Matthew 11:28), with the assurance that 'whosoever will' may come (Revelation 22:17). The natural man, however, in his own mind, 'receiveth not the things of the Spirit of God' (1 Corinthians 2:24) and chooses not to come. The Father, in His inscrutable ways, draws to Christ those whom He foreknew and made His elect. 'No man can come to me,' said Jesus, 'except the Father which has sent me draw him: and I will raise him up at the last day' (John 6:44). We cannot, in our finite mind, comprehend the infinite ways of God (Romans 11:33-36), but we can, and must, believe His Word" (Morris 1995).

ARMINIANISM

Arminian beliefs follow after Jacobus or James Arminius (1560-1609). Arminians place a strong emphasis on human freedom. God allows and expects humans to exercise the will they have been given. If this were not so, we would not find biblical invitations to choose God, the "whosoever will" passages such as "Come unto me, all ye that labour and are heavy laden, and I will give you rest" (Matt. 11:28). The very offering of such invitations implies that the hearer has the genuine possibility of either accepting or rejecting them. This, however, seems inconsistent with the position that God's decisions have rendered the future certain. If they had, there would be no point in issuing invitations to humans, for God's decisions as what would happen would come to pass regardless of what they do. The Arminians therefore look for some other way of regarding the decisions of God (Erickson 1998).

Pelagius emphasized the idea of free will. Unlike other creatures, humans were created free of controlling influences of the universe. Furthermore, humans today are free of any determining influence from the fall (Erickson 1998).

As it relates to the doctrine of predestination, the views of Arminius are quite clear and can be readily summarized. God's absolute decree regarding salvation was not the assignment of certain individuals to eternal life and others to damnation but the appointment of His Son, Jesus Christ, to be the Savior of the human race. Second, God decreed that all who repent and believe shall be saved. In addition, God has granted to all persons sufficient grace to enable them to believe. They freely believe or disbelieve on their own. God does not compel us to believe. Finally, God predestines those whom He foreknows will believe (Erickson 1998).

Election, according to Calvin, is God's choice of certain persons to His special favor. It may refer to the choice of Israel as God's special covenant people or to the choice of individuals to some special office (Erickson 1998).

In the eighteenth century, John Wesley popularized Arminianism. In fact, for many years he edited a magazine called *The Arminian*. While holding to the freedom of free will, Wesley went beyond Arminius by emphasizing the idea of prevenient or universal grace.

This universal grace is the basis of any human good in the world. This prevenient grace also makes it possible for any person to accept the offer of salvation in Jesus Christ (Wesley 1979).

In addition to understanding the difference between Calvinism and Arminianism, there should be an understanding of inerrancy and inspiration. Inspiration of the Scriptures is very clearly mentioned in two important passages in the Bible. When speaking of inspiration, the reference is that God divinely influenced writers in such a way that the very words of God were written. The word "inspiration" simply means "God-breathed," meaning that the Bible is truly the Word of God. "Now we have received, not the spirit of the world, but the spirit which is of God; that we might know the things that are freely given to us of God. Which things also we speak, not in words which man's wisdom teacheth but which the Holy Ghost teacheth; comparing spiritual things with spiritual" (1 Cor. 2:12-13). "For prophecy came not in old time by the will of man, but Holy men of God spake as they were moved by the Holy Ghost" (1 Peter 1:21). God used men with their distinctive personalities, but divinely inspired everything that they wrote.

INSPIRATION AND INERRANCY

The most clearly seen Scripture tells us that God inspired all Scripture: "All Scripture is given by inspiration of God, and is profitable for doctrine, for reproof, for correction, for instruction in righteousness that the man of God may be perfect, thoroughly furnished unto all good works" (1 Tim 3:16-17). The word used here and in the above notations refutes any idea of human inspiration. The Scriptures, by whatever particular methods God may have used in their various parts, came from spirit-guided minds (Morris 1995). As to Inerrancy, we turn to the *"Chicago Statement on Bible Inerrancy,"* formulated in October 1978 by more than 200 evangelical leaders at a conference sponsored by the International Council on Bible Inerrancy, held in Chicago, and signed by 334 highly respected signers from various evangelical Christian denominations. They included Francis Schaeffer, R. C. Sproul, Gleason Archer, Wayne Gruden, Jack Hayford, and many other well-known theologians. "The statement affirms this inerrancy of Scripture afresh, making clear our understanding of it and warning against its denial. We are persuaded that to deny it is to set aside the witness of Jesus Christ and of the Holy Spirit and to refuse the submission to the claims of God's own word which marks the true Christian faith".

The entire document is shown in Appendix I. Professor Francis L. Patton, observes,

> *If on simple historical testimony it can be proved that Jesus wrought miracles, uttered prophecies, and proclaimed His Divinity–if it can be shown that He was crucified to redeem sinners, that He rose again from the dead and that He made the destiny of men to hinge on their acceptance of Him as their Savior– then whether the records be inspired or no, woe unto him who neglects so great salvation.*

We have no need, however, to discuss this possibility further because we are not left with any doubt because we know that "All Scripture is given by inspiration of God" (2 Tim. 3:16).

The right doctrine must be taught. "It is not for a moment that we can begin to get anywhere until the right doctrines are taught. But the right doctrines mentally assented to be not an end in them, but should only be the vestibule to a personal and loving communion with God, (Letters of Francis Schaeffer). Theology is getting to know God, who He is and what He has done, so the church can grow closer to Him and to one another, yet many Christians today are proclaiming that theology is not important or needed. A church that does not want to teach theology, or is scared that it is boring, is a church that does not want to know and grow in Christ. It is a feeble and pathetic church in God's sight and worthless in the kingdom. It will be a club or a lodge and not a real effectual church. The church that you should be looking for will be a church that is alive and well (Schaeffer 2012).

CHAPTER FOUR
THE SCRIPTURES

"What is truth?" asked Pilate, and his tone inferred that the search was in vain and hopeless. If there be no authoritative guide to knowledge about God, man and the world, then Pilate was right. There is no need to grope in doubt and skepticism, for there is a Book – "the Holy Scriptures, which is able to make thee wise unto salvation through faith which is in Christ Jesus" (2 Tim. 3:15) (Pearlman 1937).

The truth can only be found in the "authoritative" Word of God. But the question may be, "why and how can we depend on the Bible for answers?" In addition to the subject previously discussed relating to the inspiration of the Scriptures, we must understand that truth abides in the Word itself. "I am the Lord, I change not" (Mal. 3:6). God is unchangeable and so is His word. "Heaven and earth shall pass away, but my words shall not pass away" (Matt. 24:35).

Since we believe that the Scriptures are clear, why are we so eager to accept changes to His Word in the form of any version of the Bible that seems to appear? There are those who claim that the inerrant Word of God is only found in the original manuscripts. Since no one has the original manuscripts, how do we know that God has preserved His Word? Did God leave us with an imperfect translation? If so, how can we know what God really said? Are the new versions more accurate and better than the old versions? Some people have that idea that new is better and therefore go with the new. If we go with the new translations, which one shall we believe? The primary question may be answered with Scripture. "But God hath revealed them unto us by His Spirit: or the Spirit searcheth all things, yea, the deep things of God. For what man knoweth the things of a man save the spirit of the man which is in him? Even so the things of God knoweth no man, but the Spirit of God. Now we have received, not the spirit of the world, but the Spirit which is of God; that we might know the things that are freely given to us of God" (1 Cor. 2:10). "But the Comforter, which is the Holy Ghost, whom the Father will send in my name, He shall teach you all things, and bring all things your remembrance, whatsoever I have said unto you"(John 14:26). "Howbeit, when He, the Spirit of truth, is come, He will guide you into all truth…" (John 16:13).

"My people are destroyed for a lack of knowledge: because thou hast rejected my knowledge, I will also reject thee, that thou shalt be no more priests to me: seeing thou hast forgotten the law of thy God, I will also forget thy children (Hosea 4:6). "Therefore My people have gone into captivity, because they have no knowledge, and their multitude dried up with thirst" (Isa. 5:13). In view of these and other similar verses, would it not be advisable to study the Scriptures with understanding? Many churches have lost the desire to teach Scripture, and are no longer advising the congregation to bring their Bibles to church. Knowledge, understanding and wisdom; these three come from God, and take precedence over all other possessions.

"Whosoever transgresseth, and abideth not in the doctrine of Christ, hath not God. He that abideth in the doctrine of Christ, he hath both the Father and the Son. If there come any unto you, and bring not this doctrine, receive him not into your house, neither bid him God speed" (2 John 9-10). This is a warning against the damage of false teachers who deny the incarnation of God in Christ Jesus. When choosing a church, ask about the doctrine of the incarnation. Also, don't abide in a church that preaches false doctrine. You know now what the church doctrine is.

The objective here is to be certain before choosing a church that leadership in that church teaches these truths. Make sure that the Bible that you use is not corrupt. Remember that the Bible is a spiritual book and is understandable to those who are led by the Spirit. Paraphrasing or attempting to change the language of Scripture will not lead to a better understanding. The Bible tells us that in the last days, there will be a falling away of the church.

INTENTIONAL ERROR

It may seem to be a strange remark to be inserted in a paper with the title, "What Kind of a Church do you Want?" But when one's desire is to find a church where the truth is preached and the messages are "tried in the fire", there must be an advisory posted when smoke is discovered. In 1963, such an advisory was posted by Mrs. Patricia Nordman and recorded in the Congressional Record. Only one of these warnings will be printed here, but an important one. Under unanimous consent, the Honorable A. S. Herlong, Jr. of Florida in the House of Representatives presented "Current Communist Goals". There were many of these goals that applied directly to religion such as presenting homosexuality as "normal, natural, and healthy"; eliminate prayer in schools and others, but the one that is most disturbing was article number 27: "Infiltrate the churches and replace "revealed" religion with "social" religion. Discredit the Bible and emphasize the need for intellectual maturity, which does not need a "religious crutch."

The entire document, forty-five articles, was placed in the Congressional Record, Vol. 109, 88th Congress, 1st Session Appendix Pages A1-A2842 Jan. 9-May 7, 1963 Reel 12. This is not to say that the United States is under some kind of Communist control, but what should be noted is that of the forty-five issues listed; nearly all of them have come to pass. On June 17, 1963, the Supreme Court concluded that any Bible reciting or prayer, in public schools, was deemed unconstitutional.

"There is a problem in the church today as theology is ignored and good doctrine disappears or is watered down from the pulpit and the airways, and is replaced by what 'feels good' or what we feel is needed is Christian junk food. When theology disappears from the church and its leaders, there will be a free for all of what we think is truth. The situation will be created where God is moved to the back seat to the god of self or of the favored trend of the day as the central focus of our faith and that will carve a road to hell" (Schaeffer 2012).

A church without theology is a church without God, as theology is about knowing who God is and what He has done for us. A theology without a Sovereign God is simply not an option for the church or daily faith, because He is being replaced with us or idols or false teachings (Schaeffer 2012).

"Ye are of God, little children, and have overcome them: because greater is He that is in you than he that is in the world" (1 John 4:4). Even though this Scripture is known and quoted frequently, there is still a perceived notion that what we have is not what this world wants. The belief is that they will not be attracted to what we have unless they can see it for themselves.

In 605 BC, the Babylonians invaded Jerusalem. Instead

of destroying the nation, Babylon decided to destroy Israel's identity and culture. They turned Israel in a slave state. In the process of doing so, they selected the most promising children of Israel and shipped them off to be immersed into Babylonian culture. At least four of these children were taken to the king's palace. The king gave them new names and taught them new languages. All changes were acceptable, except to Daniel, who drew the line when the king appointed a different food. He saw that he would be forced to eat meat offered to idols. Daniel requested a different diet, obtaining permission from the king with the understanding that they would be healthier at the end of the trial period. The lesson learned is that when confronted with a test that supresses Scriptural doctrine, God will provide a way (Smith 2012).

Before selecting that church, be certain that the world has not infiltrated it. Be armed with the sword of truth.

GOD'S PEOPLE DESTROYED?

"My people are destroyed for lack of knowledge: because thou hast rejected knowledge, I will also reject thee…" (Hosea 4:6). "Therefore my people have gone into captivity, because they have no knowledge…" (Isa. 5:13). This indicates that God's people are physically and mentally being destroyed and literally go into captivity as a result of not having adequate knowledge. A perfect example of this destruction is the Muslim suicide bombers, many being young children. They have been indoctrinated to believe in a false religion and literally are being brought into captivity. The reverse is also true. Adequate knowledge of God can keep one out of serious trouble when looking for that church. Knowledge, wisdom and understanding come directly from God. Use the knowledge that God will provide for you. "The simple believeth every word, but the prudent man looketh well to his going" (Pro. 14:15). God wants you to stop, think and be careful in evaluating your choices.

OLD AND NEW

One identifying mark of a good church is found in the pulpit. The best of churches teach from both the Old Testament and the New Testament, and exegetical preaching and teaching provides a better understanding. Some teach only from the New Testament indicating that since Jesus came, the Old Testament is no longer material. This improper doctrine is included in liberal scholarship. When teaching what is known as the "documentary theory", the historical evidence is lost, thereby losing the entire flow. Many liberal Bible colleges and seminaries teach that there is no importance in Old

Testament study. Teaching the entire Bible as the Word of God, provides understanding of categories such as the sacrifice and shedding of blood.

The divisions of both the Old Testament and the New Testament are important. The Old Testament begins with the Law, a basic understanding of how sinners can be made acceptable to a Holy God. The Prophets are very important to understand because they are expositors with a clear view of what is to be. The Writings include the very poetic truth of God with implication of wisdom and power. The Book of Proverbs, for example, provides the very best of counseling, exceeding any other books ever written.

When people are not receiving sound Biblical doctrine, they are usually not aware of the loss (J. A. Motyer 2000).

CHAPTER FIVE
WHY GO TO CHURCH?

"I don't see the point of church," one man said. "I just prefer my independent Bible study. Organized religion just doesn't make sense to me." This is typical of what could be classified as "alternative churches." The Bible says, "And let us consider one another to provoke unto love and to good works: Not forsaking the assembling of ourselves together, as the manner of some is; but exhorting one another: and so much more, as ye see the day approaching (Heb. 10:24-25).

In a Greenville News, Greenville, SC article, quoting from a Washington Post article entitled "More Christians opting for In-home Services" (June 10, 2006), Michael Alison Chandler and Arianne Aryanpur discussed how many thousands were finding alternative churches. George Barna, a religion pollster, estimates that since the year 2000, more than 20 million Americans have begun exploring alternative forms of worship including home churches, workplace ministries, and online faith communities. Barna himself is a home- churcher. In this article, an in-home alternative church is described as no preacher, no sermon, and no pastor-led prayers. When it came time to bow their heads, each of ten adults had something to contribute. One man prayed for success with his new fitness program. One comment was that you can't ask questions in church.

Martin Luther wrote in the Smalacald Articles (III, XII), "Thank God a seven-year old child knows what a church is, namely holy believers and sheep who hear the voice of their Shepherd." Jesus said, "My sheep hear my voice and I know them, and they follow me. And I give them eternal life, and they shall never perish" (John 10:27-28).

Since the church is the assembly of saints in which the Gospel is taught and the sacraments are administered rightly, should there be questions relating to the validity of going to church? Paul's advice to the church is to encourage one another by meeting together (Heb.10:25). The Bible instructs believers to be in relationship with other believers: "So we, being many, are one body in Christ and every one members one of another" (Rom. 12:5). When church attendance is taken casually, spiritual growth is in jeopardy.

In the German language, a word that is often mistranslated as "worship" is the word "Gottesdienst." which means literally "Divine Service." often called the Liturgy, which comes from the Greek word for service. Divine Service is what should be going on when church service is the agenda (Pearlman 1937).

"Two men went up to the temple to pray, one a Pharisee and the other a tax collector" (Luke 18:10).

In this famous parable of Jesus, the Pharisee attends a praise service at which he thanks God for "gifting" him and thus making him better than his fellows. The tax collector attends the Divine Service. He cries out for mercy. The tax collector went home justified, Jesus tells us. That is, he went home forgiven of his sins. He received the mercy for which he pleaded. This plea for mercy is the presupposition of the Divine Service. "If you cannot or will not sing The Kyrie" (meaning Lord, a common name in an important prayer of Christian liturgy), you cannot be served by God nor can you be saved" (Preus 2000).

CONCERNING SPIRITUAL GIFTS

The gifts of the Spirit must be distinguished from the gift of the Spirit. The former describes the supernatural abilities imparted by the Spirit for special ministries; the latter refers the impartation of the Spirit to believers as ministered by the ascended Christ (Acts 2:33).

Paul speaks of the gifts of the Spirit ("Spirituals" in the *Textus Receptus*), is a threefold aspect. They are "charismata," or a variety of gifts conferred by the one Spirit (1 Cor. 12:4, 7); "diakonai," or varieties of services rendered in the cause of one Lord; and "energemata" or varieties of the power of the one God who works all in all. All these aspects are referred to as "the manifestation of the Spirit," which is given to men for the profit of all.

The main purpose of the gifts of the Spirit, discounted by many, is Spiritual enablements for the purpose of building up the church of God through the instruction of believers and the winning of converts. Paul enumerates nine of these gifts in 1Cor. 12:8-10, which may be classified as follows:

1. Those that impart power to know supernaturally: the word of wisdom, the word of knowledge, discernment.
2. Those that impart power to act supernaturally: faith, miracles, healings.
3. Those that impart power to speak supernaturally: prophecy, tongues, interpretation.

These gifts are described as "the manifestation of the Spirit, given to every man to profit withal" (that is for the benefit of the church).

Many churches deny that Spiritual gifts are in effect today and were given only to the disciples and the church on the day of Pentecost. The comfort level in a church that includes the doctrine of the Holy Spirit gifts in accordance with 1 Cor. 12:1-10 in conformity with verse 28, "And God hath set some in the church, first apostles, secondarily prophets, thirdly teachers, after that, miracles, then the gifts of healings, helps, governments, diversities of tongues," is important in choosing a church. If the purpose of the impartation of the gifts of the Spirit, is as described above, and the church disregards these gifts as not to be applied today, then verses 28 through 31 also must be discounted and deemed not applicable. Some would disassemble verse 28 and only include "teachers" as applicable for today.

CHAPTER SIX
LEAVING A CHURCH

Included in previous chapters, are various types of worship, dealing primarily with doctrinal issues. Before looking for that special church, many questions should be asked, both of the seeker and of the potential church.

Several primary questions should be answered by members in the potential church. Are members satisfied with the current spiritual aspects of the church? Is the church growing spiritually? Is attendance increasing or decreasing? Are members being added consistently? Are the finances of the church stable? Are members leaving and if so, why?

A recent poll of members leaving churches resulted in the following:

1. Dissatisfaction with the pastor — 40%
2. The music is not to our liking — 24%
3. We prefer a more formal atmosphere — 8%
4. There is no reverence in the church before and after the service — 8%
5. The teaching/preaching includes more of the "milk" of the Word, instead of the "meat" — 5%
6. Church appears to be in the entertainment business — 5%

7. Lack of exegetical preaching   5%
8. Not a "serious" atmosphere   5%
(Telephone calls to 100 random individuals Jan. 2010-Dec. 2010)

More than one in five adults who switch to a new church move away from traditional worship, a study revealed. In a series of studies on adults who switch churches, Lifeway Research found "church switchers" often choose a new church that is different in several ways from their previous church. Most do not end up attending traditional services as they formerly did.

According to the study, 53% of church switchers attended traditional style worship. Of that, only 29% switched to churches that hold traditional services. The most popular worship styles among church switchers are blended worship (38 percent) and contemporary worship (33 percent).

"Clearly, selecting a new church with a more contemporary worship style is a current trend," said Scott McConnell, associate director of Lifeway Research, in the report. "These changes are intentional, as indicated by eighty percent finding a worship style an important factor in selecting a new church."

The study also found that nearly half (46 percent) of those who switch churches, move to a larger church. Meanwhile, 29 percent switch to a smaller church and

25 percent choose a church the same size as their former church. Among those who attend a church with 100 or less people, 79 percent switched to a larger church. Among people who attended a church with more than 500 in worship attendance, 57 percent moved to a smaller church.

"The trend clearly shows church switchers are moving to larger churches," McConnell noted in the report. "However, there is a smaller counter-trend among those who attend larger churches; some of them selected smaller new churches. Results from the study backed previous studies that revealed lack of loyalty to a denomination.

Fifty-four percent of church switchers change denominations when moving to a new church, the latest Lifeway study found. Forty-four percent of church switchers consider denomination as an important factor is selecting a church.

The high rate of change in denomination is actually an indication of how few church switchers value denomination" McConnell noted.

"Other factors drive the church selection decision, and most people give less consideration to denomination."

Among churchgoers who have disagreements with their previous church's teachings or positions on issues, 71 percent of them change denominations. The study showed that only 4 percent of church switchers say one of the reasons they left their previous church is they could no longer identify with that particular denomination (Barrick 2007).

ANOTHER VIEW

According to Eryn Sun, *Christian Post Reporter*, many churches today have become too obsessed with youth culture: idolizing whatever is new, fresh, and cutting edge, particularly in the area of worship.

Concerned that a kind of "celebrity culture" was permeating into worship, detracting from Christ and His vision for a church, three experienced worship leaders came together on *The Gospel Coalition* to talk about implications of the growing phenomenon and address ways that the church could challenge those idolatries.

"I see congregations where there is such an attachment to all of the entrapments of youth in America and this fundamental belief that we're not going to get old or that we can be both old and young at the same time," Isaac Wardell, the worship director of Trinity Presbyterian Church, shared. "Churches are stuck in a mentality that worship had to be constantly newer, fresher, and the next best thing, oftentimes losing focus on the message of the Gospel as a result.

The idolatries with youth culture, which had led to the selection of young, hip and extremely talented worship leaders, inevitably cause many congregants to feel inadequate as well, discouraging them from using their gifts because they do not feel they "looked, dressed, or sounded the part."

"It has nothing to do with a local congregation," Mike Cosper, the pastor of worship and arts at Sojourn Community Church, noted. "It has everything to do with this machine that's being driven in there."

Illustrating a practical example of the "machine" in question, Wardell explained how when he first came to his own church in Virginia, he found that their whole worship volunteer team was between the ages of 25 to 36, even though the congregation was made up of many different age groups.

"One of the things we said right away within the first year of our church's worship ministry was to say we're going to actively start recruiting people to be involved with our worship program that are not in the (25-36 years old) demographic," the Bifrost Arts director shared.

During their recruiting process, they would also clearly explain what being a worship leader was and was not.

"(We tried) to encourage our church musicians to get outside of that onstage experience, of being in front of everybody with microphones and actually saying part of being a worship leader is...(working) with the children...(going) to nursing homes and (leading) worship there," and so forth, he explained. (Sun 2012)

CONTEMPORARY (CHRISTIAN) MUSIC DEFINED

The genre that would be eventually known as Contemporary Christian music came from the Jesus movement revival of the latter 1960s and early 1970s, and was originally called "Jesus music." "About that time, many young people from the sixties' counterculture professed to believe in Jesus. Convinced of the bareness of a lifestyle based on drugs, free sex, and radical politics, 'hippies' became 'Jesus people'. Of course there were people who felt like Jesus was another "trip." "The 'Jesus movement' of the 1970s was when things really started changing, and Christian music began to become an industry within itself." "Jesus Music" started by playing instruments and singing songs about love and peace, which translated into love of God. Paul Wohlegemuth, who wrote the book "Rethinking the Church" said, "(the) 1970s will see a marked acceptance of rock-influenced music in all levels of church music. The rock style will become more familiar to all people, its rhythmic excesses will become refined, and its earlier secular associations will be less remembered" (Baker 1985).

An article in the *Greenville News*, Greenville, S.C., June 10, 2006 by Tom Schaefer stated, "Many people who once claimed a traditional Christian faith have left it or have reshaped it. For example, Michael Wall of Salem, S.C., a former church member now believes that Jesus Christ was a wonderful teacher with a wise and wonderful message for mankind, but organized religions are too focused on doctrinaire details, which detracts from the essence of their message and leads to schism and conflict." This is typical of those who have heard the Gospel but reject it. If Jesus was not God, He was a deceiver, not a wonderful teacher. How could a teacher be accepted as a wonderful teacher if he is a deceiver? While a number of people have pretended to possess extraordinary insight and capabilities, in due time, almost always within their lifetime, their pretensions have become all too apparent. Jesus' teachings have stood the test of time, and have never been shown to be anything except the way, the truth, and the life (Crout 2006).

"And be not conformed to this world: but be transformed by the renewing of your mind, that ye may prove what is that good, and acceptable, and perfect will, of God" (Romans 12:2).

"People sometimes ask me why I am opposed, in principle, to the use of guitars for music in church, and in general, why I think that musical contemporary styles are incompatible with the spirit of the liturgy. My first answer is perhaps a weaker argument, an argument from authority: an eminent theologian who has written deeply and clearly on liturgy, Joseph Ratzinger, holds this opinion and defends it persuasively. But my second answer, my own explanation, is based on my personal experience with church music. Whether the tunes are sentimental or snappy makes no difference—it is nothing other than a conforming of our minds to our secularized age, to the artistic, psychological, and spiritual degeneracy of our times. It is a sort of aping of Bob Dylan and Billy Joel. It is as if the mass marketed 'rock anthem' is implicitly recognized as a new standard of excellence, to which even music for the worship of God must be conformed" (Kwasniewski 2005).

The opinions above are examples of diversities of standards of worship. As indicated above, a majority of moves from one church to another are moves related to the contemporary style of worship. All signs point to the desire for something new, whether or not Scriptural, or as in the above article, a "new standard of excellence." This new casual approach to church should be analyzed carefully. Conformation to the world is widely separated from transformation. An article in the Greenville News, Greenville, S.C. on May 27, 2006 was entitled, "A New Spirit to Mainline Church." "The pews have been replaced by upholstered chairs in St. Paul's Lutheran Church. The altar is now an expansive stage that accommodates drummers, guitarist, and keyboard players. The most popular seats in the building are the two leather couches that make the church's entryway feel like a hip coffee shop. St. Paul rocks with dancing, clapping, and happy music that is making its contemporary services ever more popular, eclipsing the traditional Sunday morning services it still offers. The church is just looking for a way to speak to culture."

Be absolutely certain whether this "conformation" is the proper way to move.

THE CHOICES

At this position in looking for a church, there are other questions that should be answered before beginning visits to other churches:

WHAT KIND OF CHURCH DO YOU NEED?

According to Andrew Doran (First Things), Oscar Wilde once observed that "the Catholic Church is for saints and sinners alone. For respectable people, the Anglican Church will do." The pastor of Grace Lutheran Church in Clarksville, TN, added that Newt Gingrich would have made a pitiable Anglican—or Mormon, for that matter. As a Catholic, however, he fits right in. Catholics are all too familiar with frailty, and in fact the central idea of redemption by Christ presupposes a need for such redemption.

The churches that preach sin and repentance, grace and forgiveness are often seen as out of step for "respectable" folks only because the "respectable" folks don't talk in those terms or think in those categories. The quote would certainly have to be redone today. Perhaps the Anglican Church would do for those who like the appearance of traditional Christianity but the rest of the crowd would be better suited for other places. Those who think religion is mostly morality might probable like the Mormon Church. Those who think religion is mostly about happy lives and good feelings might better turn to Lakewood or Osteen. You can continue the list, but Oscar Wilde hits it on the mark. The Evangelical and the Catholic faith are about redemption for sinners, righteousness for the evil, cleansing for the guilty, life for the dying, and hope for those who know they cannot repair what is wrong with them or in the world.

If the church is out of step, or appears to be out of step, it just might be because that church is being faithful to the Gospel. Don't worry about being relevant but about being faithful, about what goes on in worship, about striving about what is best for Him who gave us all. If what it takes to fill pews requires unfaithfulness, then let us rejoice at the remnant in the pews and preach with the vigor and honesty of Stephen. Even if we see no change in the statistics, we will have done what God calls us to do. And, in the end, this is the only approval that matters (Peters 2012).

WHAT KIND OF CHURCH DOES JESUS WANT? (John 17)

If you really want to know what the Lord desires in a church, turn to Chapter 17 of John. His Word to the church is an expression of His desires for His people. His intercessory prayer provides us with the clearest picture of a perfect church.

"And now I am no more in the world, and I come to Thee, Holy Father, keep through Thine own name those whom Thou hast given me, that they may be one, as we are" (John 17:11). Jesus' prayer is that we remain loyal to God, walking in full adherence to God's character. Jesus wanted a church that acted like God that would think, live, and speak the same as He did. His desire is one of unity, a unity of love for one another and for God. The primary purpose for church attendance is that we might be one. All other reasons are not reasons at all but are things that we do.

"That they all may be one; as Thou, Father, art in me, and I in Thee, that they also may be one in us: that the world may believe that Thou hast sent me" (John 17:21). Jesus wants us to walk in unity as a witness to the gospel and a perfectly unified church as that the world would

know that God sent Him.

"These things have I spoken to you, that my joy might remain in you, and that your joy might be full" (John 15:11). Joy is a state of gladness. Some professing Christians appear to have no joy in their lives. Sin destroys Christian joy. Jesus wanted a church that is filled with the fear of God, radical unity, and an intense joy and zest for life.

In the Lord's Prayer, the verse that said, "Deliver us from evil" is asking for protection for the church and the individual. One difficulty is found in some of the new versions of the Bible, adding the word, "from the evil one;" which is not in any Greek text. In the Greek, "evil" is *tou ponerou*, literally "the evil." Some may have the opinion that there is no difference, but Satan is not omnipotent nor is he omnipresent. "The devil made me do it!" is totally unscriptural, so the proper translation is stated in the King James Version. It is the little sins that we pay no attention to.

Jesus wants the church to be separated and set apart from the world by a radical devotion to the Word of God. Rather than adopting the things of the world and actually bringing them into the church, He wants the church to be set apart (sanctified). How the church is separated from the world, may be an important question to ask.

"A new commandment I give unto you that ye love one

another; as I have loved you that ye also love one another. By this shall all men know that ye are my disciples if ye have love one to another" (John 13:34-35). There is no greater love than that the Father has for His Son. Jesus wanted a church filled with His love.

Love is patient with others; love is kind to others and is not jealous. Love does not brag; and is not arrogant. Love does not act unbecomingly. (this means that love does not bring shame on the Christian community). Love seeks not its own; is not self-centered; is not provoked (provoke not anger).

In summary, Jesus wants a church that walks in the fear of God, one that is perfectly united in truth, a church that is walking in sanctification, separate from the world, filled with His complete joy, and completely immersed in His love. Holiness, unity, joy, sanctification, and love are the things Jesus wants to see in His church, according to His prayer in Chapter 17 of John. There is certainly more that He requires, but these attributes are the ones that made it in His prayer, and most, if not all, of the other things that one should find in the church that Jesus wants.

"For if these things be in you, and abound, they make you that ye shall neither be barren nor unfruitful in the knowledge of our Lord Jesus Christ" (2 Peter 1:8). The key here is "true knowledge." A true knowledge of Jesus Christ translates into a true hunger and pursuit of God.

Such a church is the kind of church that Jesus wants. What are you doing to be that church? Such a church begins with individual leaders whose lives reflect these very qualities. They lead others into these qualities by example, by teaching, and by preaching.

Martin Luther displayed a life of character and goodness in his life that few others ever did. He loved God and was willing to die for truth. The truth of God will move His church into the place where Jesus wanted it. May we seek the truth, and as He opens our eyes, let us repent and apply it to our lives so that we become the bride that Jesus wants. The mercies of the Lord endure forever. Repentance is a lifestyle, not an isolated act (Dingess 2011).

WHAT KIND OF GOD DO YOU WANT?

A man asked his son does he know who God is. The little boy answered, "I sure do. He's the one who lives in heaven looking down to find the people who are having fun so He can stop them". Most people want a powerless God who leaves them alone. That is, until a crisis comes along. Most churches at that time want a mini-revival, just to get God to come down and get things in order.

Practicing Jews want a powerful God, the Messiah, who will restore rulership in the world to them. Just like the question the disciples asked Jesus, "Lord, wilt thou at this time restore again the kingdom of Israel?"(Acts 1:6).

The Muslims plan on a powerful God. They want God to come down and do something, and they're ready to die for it.

Christians want a God that leaves them alone. Did you ever notice at about 11:30 on Sunday morning how people get nervous when the service lasts too long? Christians want a kind of "pat on the back" short sermons, not one that calls God down in a whirlwind. They want the world and all of its fun and to be left alone. Just read the Scriptures and find out what happens when God gives them what they want.

They wanted meat because they were tired of manna in the desert, so He gave it to them until they were sick. They wanted a king, so He gave them one and let them deal with all the consequences. The city where the demoniac was healed asked Jesus to leave them alone. He did! God got back in the boat and sailed away.

When the church wants God more than anything else, He will give it to them, but not before. (What kind of God do you want, Gray 2011).

WOULD JESUS ATTEND YOUR CHURCH?

If Jesus walked the earth today, what kind of church would He attend? "And seek not what ye shall eat, or what ye shall drink, neither be ye of doubtful mind. For all these things do the nations of the world seek after: and *your Father* knoweth that ye have need of these things. But rather seek ye the kingdom of God; and all these things shall be added unto you" (Luke 12:29-31). This doctrine that Jesus taught is to be applied both to the individual and to the church.

If Jesus came to your door on Sunday morning and inquired about your church, He may inform you of the reason for His visit. The visit will only be for a short time, about three hours, and informs you that He is considering going to your church. Since its "Friend Day" the pastor will be overwhelmed at your visitor. What will He find? The church doors are open and services are held at least three times weekly. The building is beautiful, perfectly adorned with the best of furniture, stained glass windows, and perfect in every way.

Jesus smiles and says, "I know your Father has been here before, but I want to go to a church where there is the greatest need. There are homeless people close by, castaways of all sorts and during my short visit to earth, I want to meet with them. Will they be here?"

If your answer is no, maybe there needs to be a re-evaluation of the purpose of the church. Your church has fellowship, discipleship, meets the needs of your members, but "Pure religion and undefiled before God and the Father is this: To visit the fatherless, and widows in their affliction, and to keep himself unspotted from the world" (James 1:27).

We go to church to be fed spiritually but the mission of the church is to feed. There is nothing wrong with what the above church is doing, but the priorities need to be observed.

The story is told of Florence Chadwick who, at the age of 34, conquered the English Channel, but when she attempted to swim the Catalina Channel, the day was extremely foggy and the water was cold. After almost 16 hours, she gave up and got into the boat, not realizing that shore was only a half-mile away. Later on, she tried again, facing the same obstacles, but she knew what her goal was and completed her task.

The understanding of the teachings of Christ must take precedence if we are to accomplish the will of the Father in our church. The need is to stay out of the fog if possible, but at least know where the fog is. Know where the goal is.

Where would Jesus attend church? Would He attend where praises are sung, but have little influence on the members' daily choices? Would He attend where Jesus is Savior but not master? Where God's dominion and laws are replaced with the acceptance that every person determines right or wrong for his or her own life? Or would He be looking for a church where people are striving to submit to God's dominion in their daily lives and seeking His kingdom? *Of course, the real question is not "Would Jesus attend my church?" But, rather, "Am I attending Jesus' church?"* (Petty 2012)

CHAPTER SEVEN
CHOOSING A CHURCH

It takes a considerable amount of time and persistence to find the church you are looking for. There are questions that should be answered in the process of finding that church that God wants you to find.

There should be a basic understanding of the church type. As previously seen, the core theology of the church will determine the value of the prospective church.

- If you believe that the Roman Catholic Church is the true church, then your search will be limited. It's not unlikely that you will end up at the church closest to where you live.
- If you think of church primarily as a place for theological input, then you will be more inclined to seek strong preaching and teaching, and to make this a priority.
- If you think of church more as a body of believers who share life and ministry together, then you are less worried about the quality of the preaching and more interested in finding a church with strong fellowship.

Choosing a church is one of the most important things you will do in a lifetime. A good church will help shape your life and your relationship to God. The choice is important and the choices are countless. Be certain before choosing a church that you understand the doctrine of that church and that it conforms to your principles. For example, if you believe that the Bible is written under the inspiration of the Holy Spirit and the first sermon you hear denies the inspiration of Scriptures, you may be in the wrong church. Every church should be about the worship of God because that defines the very point of existence. Worship is not sitting through a worship service and singing songs. Intimate communication with God is the real purpose. The church should assist you in all walks of life, not just on Sunday. Sound doctrine needs to be in the church. There are a lot of false doctrines in many churches. According to Scripture, there is just one faith: "There is one body, and one Spirit, even as ye are called in one hope of your calling: One Lord, one faith, one baptism, One God and Father of all, who is above all, and through all, and in you all. But unto every one of us is given grace according to the measure of the gift of Christ" (Eph. 4:4-7).

Most good churches post a doctrinal statement either in the church, on their website, or both. Observe this statement and see if it agrees with Scripture. If there is a question, verify with a good source. Scripture verifies Scripture without error.

Good fellowship should not be the objective of a

church. Even though a lot of good things result in social gatherings, consider: "And let us consider one another, to provoke unto love and to good works" (Heb. 10:24); and "As every man hath received the gift, even so minister the same one to another, as good stewards of the manifold grace of God" (1 Pet.4:10). Jesus demonstrated the importance of fellowship when He invested His life into the twelve apostles and sent them out to do His work.

Expository preaching confers belief in the authority of Scripture. This is the oldest form of preaching, and it will never go out of style. This is the type preaching that explains the Scriptures, explaining the meaning and the application. Martin Luther was earnestly seeking to understand Scripture and what he heard did not match up to the words he was reading. Don't check your Bible at the door, but follow what the preacher is saying in your Bible and confirm what is being taught. Sometimes one word deviation in the reading of Scripture from the pulpit or from a teacher can change the entire context of the teaching.

The Bible is the authoritative Word of God, trumping everything else. In church life, this means that the Bible should be the authoritative source for preaching and teaching. It should guide the decisions of church leaders in a way unparalleled by any other authority.

There are authorities that compete with that of

Scripture. Historically, one such authority has been church tradition. Some Christians believe that church tradition stands on par with the Bible when it comes to authority in the church, and even above the Bible. Church tradition has much to offer, but the Bible supersedes all others. In many cases, church tradition and the Bible agree, but when there is a difference, the Bible takes precedence.

Another competing authority is that of church leaders. This can be found not only in the Roman Catholic Church but in others as well. For example, what is expressed through the Pope can establish doctrine on par with Scripture, even if there is no Biblical evidence to support that doctrine. There are some Roman Catholic churches that teach the Bible as absolute authority, so if the inclination is toward Catholicism, look for those parishes that support Scripture as authoritative.

Another competitor for Biblical authority is personal experiences and feelings. Many churches teach now that homosexuality is accepted because they interpret Scripture making it acceptable (1 Cor. 6:9-10). Truth, however, trumps all else. Romans 1:25 warns of those who changed the truth of God into a lie and worshiped and served the creature more than the creator.

One of the primary callings of the church is to evangelize, proclaiming the news that those who don't know the truth will hear and believe. There are many churches that don't preach the gospel of salvation through the death and resurrection of Christ, simply because they don't believe it. Many believe that just preaching the love of God and His acceptance of all people and doctrines is adequate.

Religious tolerance is not Biblical. Jesus said, "I am the way, the truth and the life, and no one comes to the Father except by me" (John 14:6). Acceptance of another way is incorrect doctrine.

Make certain that one of the primary characteristics of the church is orthodox (that word means "right believing"). What constitutes orthodoxy are such basics as: God as Trinity; Jesus is fully God and fully human, and Jesus is the Savior of the world. Essentially, the church should be right-believing in the essential core of doctrine that has to do with the nature of God, Christ, and salvation.

Churches have to do with all sorts of wonderful things: friendship, helping the poor, music, art, teaching, prayer, and so forth. But every church must be grounded upon and centered in God who is Father, Son, and Holy Spirit, the God who became human in Jesus Christ in order to save the world. If the church is based on something other than God and God's salvation in Christ, the church is not essentially orthodox.

Before your search begins, you will probably have a list of top priorities in your mind. A fantastic public speaker with plenty of jokes and stories and great PowerPoint demonstrations may be a priority, but preaching good theology with something good to say every week may be advantageous.

Many pastors in large churches are members of what is known as "The Internet Evangelism Coalition." Their advice: don't sound preachy; avoid words like ministry, salvation, redemption, or even faith. Draw non-believers to Jesus by presenting the church as an upbeat, uplifting community of friends (Internet Evangelism Coalition 2006).

"But though we, or an angel from heaven, preach any other gospel unto you than that which we have preached unto you, let him be accursed. As we said before, so say I now again, if any man preach any other gospel to you than that ye have received, let him be accursed. For do I now persuade men or God? or do I seek to please men? For if I yet pleased men, I should not be a servant of Christ (Gal. 1:8-10). Do these verses measure up with the view of a pastor who said, "We need to offer something different?"

Take the advice from Scripture that says, "And I will give them one heart, and I will put a new spirit within you; and I will take the stony heart out of their flesh, and I will give them a heart of flesh; that they may walk in my statutes, and keep mine ordinances, and do them; and they shall be my people, and I will be their God. But as for them whose heart walketh after their detestable things and their abominations, I will recompense their way upon their own heads, saith the LORD GOD" (Ezek. 11:19-21).

The challenge is to the expression "casual worship". Real worship is never casual but it is continually in the heart of a Christian. Christianity is not a religion but a way of life and therefore can never be part time or casual. A person either follows Christ or doesn't. I submit that if the altar has been removed, there is dancing instead of kneeling, off the wall empty words on the silver screen as observed by aforementioned article, taking the place of hymns whose writers were led by the Holy Spirit, then I submit that this new spirit is not holy.

What has been described is not a style of worship, but a worship conforming to the world by allowing the world into the church and calling it worship. It may in fact be worship, but not worship of our Lord Jesus Christ who came to take away the sin of the world. We are commanded to not be conformed to the world, but "Be ye transformed by the renewing of your mind, that ye may prove what is that good and acceptable and perfect will of God" (Rom. 12:2).

Notice the word "perfect" in that verse. It does not indicate what is allowable, as misinterpreted by many, but it dictates the perfect will of God. Matthew Henry comments that "it concerns Christians to prove what is that will of God which is good and acceptable, and perfect" (Notes in Matthew Henry's commentary on Romans 12:2).

In choosing a church, the question should be, "What kind of service would you prefer to be in should Jesus return to earth on Sunday where you attend?" Would you like to be in the church that has the popular version of worship or one that truly honors Christ with "real worship", or would you prefer to be kneeling or dancing? Would your iPad, cell phone, or Bible be preferred? Would you like to be singing "happy songs" or Amazing Grace? Does it really make any difference?

In his book review of *Street Saints: Renewing America's Cities*, James Peterson said, "The most striking aspect of Elliot's book is the contrast that springs to mind, implied but not bluntly stated, between Christianity of cheap grace (in theologian Dietrich Bonhoeffer's term) and the Christianity of the changed heart. All too many of today's churches provide mere lip-service to the Christian life, providing entertaining spectacles and shallow and catchy songs, all geared toward a Christian life that bears little relation to the transcendent of the Gospel" (Elliott 2004).

"And what concord hath Christ with Be'li-al? Or what part hath he that believeth with an infidel? And what agreement hath the temple of God with Idols? For ye are the temple of the living God; as God hath said, I will dwell in them, and be ye separate, saith the Lord, and touch not the unclean thing and I will receive you" (2 Cor. 6:15-17). As a well-known Baptist evangelist Vance Havner has said, "God does not desire idle worship, or idol worship, but ideal worship".

If there is a family, they should be involved in a decision to find a new church. Is music important, and if so, what kind of music is preferable? One may like contemporary music but make certain the music is in accordance with Biblical doctrine. "It is interesting to note that in the area of music, a strict view did prevail. The reason for the disappearance of traditions of Roman musical practices in the beginning of the middle ages was that the church looked with indignation on the social occasions and pagan religious exercises connected with them. And thus, old Roman musical traditions disappeared" (Schaeffer, How Should We Then Live 1976).

Even though Emperor Constantine ended the persecution of Christians, Christianity became at first (in 313) a legal religion, then (in 381) the official state religion. In considering the culture of the Middle Ages, we must not overlook its music. Pope Gregory I brought the music of the Western church into a systematic whole. This impersonal, mystical, and other worldly music is named after him: The Gregorian Chant or plainsong, a monophony. Officially sponsored art was decadent and music was increasingly bombastic (inflated, high-sounding) (Schaeffer 1976). From about 1100-1300 there were the troubadours, a title which means inventors or finders, and they were mainly aristocrat poet-musicians of Southern France who inaugurated a flowers of secular music.

"This church as well as thousands of others across the nation is acting out skits and has replaced kneeling with dancing and replaced hymnbooks with off the wall words created by money hungry Contemporary Christian Musicians omitting the Blood of Christ 90 percent of the time. Scripture often still plays a role but only in less formalized readings. There is no need to carry your Bible (to church) anymore because the Scripture is also on the board" (Greenville News, Greenville SC May 27, 2006). Before choosing a church, determine whether or not the Gospel is being preached. If a family has children, it may be a priority that good leadership in youth is essential. Be certain, however, that what is taught in youth ministry is also Scriptural.

In selecting a church, all serious Christians will reject the typical American hedonistic, self-centered approach to choosing a church and instead will search the Scriptures in order to see how God defines a true church. When we examine the Bible we will note that there is one primary mark of a true church and two other marks that are dependent on and naturally follow the first mark. (Berkhof 1941). The primary mark of a true church is pure preaching and profession of the Word. A true church must preach true apostolic doctrine. It must preach the pure doctrine of the gospel. The two secondary marks are the lawful administration of the sacraments and the proper exercising of church discipline.

The necessity of finding a church that believes the Bible and sincerely desires to put it into practice is one of the most important attractions. The Word of God, not the pastors' own opinion, is a requirement. "The things that thou hast heard of me among many witnesses (the Apostles' doctrine), the same (not something else) commit thou to faithful men, who shall be able to teach others also" (2 Tim. 2:2).

Look for a conservative, Bible-believing church, not one based upon what it can offer me in terms of a worship style because our tastes cannot govern the living God. Much of the common advice regarding choosing a church is humanism. A popular Christian magazine recently offered this advice regarding choosing a church: "The key in choosing a worship style lies in realizing what works for you. Which form of worship: formal, spontaneous, or somewhere in between helps you best appreciate God and most enhances your Spiritual life." One factor that wasn't even considered was, What does God think about all this? Is God pleased with the church's worship? We shall all appear before the judgment seat of Christ, and what will matter then is not how good a church made you feel but whether God was pleased.

One woman wrote, "I was drawn to Mission Valley Church by the worship service. They offered a contemporary service with drama, contemporary-sounding music, and other elements that fit in with the lifestyle of people my age. The services reflect our needs and interests." This is a self-entered, not God centered approach and is therefore wrong.

Here are some questions you might want to ask the pastor. All questions anticipate a "yes" answer.
- Do you believe the Bible to be the inspired Word of God, the authoritative rule of faith and practice?
- Do you believe the Bible to be without error in matters of science and history as well as faith and doctrine?
- As the pastor, do you see it as your primary duty in preaching to explain and apply to your hearers the message of the text of the Scripture?
- Do you believe the sinner is justified by faith in Jesus Christ alone, apart from all good works?
- Do you believe in a literal hell or lake of fire in which all those who reject Jesus Christ will be punished eternally?
- Do you believe that there is no salvation for any person apart from faith in Jesus Christ?
- Do you believe that God created all things out of nothing in six literal 24-hour days?

- Do you believe in the virgin birth and miracles of Jesus Christ?
- Must God's people in this age keep the Ten Commandments in obedience to our Lord?
- Must God's people in this age observe the Christian Sabbath in obedience to Christ, the Lord of the Sabbath?
- Do you believe that the purpose of worship is to glorify God by doing only those things that He has appointed in His Word? Note: the Biblical elements of worship are prayer, Scripture reading, singing praises to God, giving tithes and offerings, preaching, the proper administration of baptism and the Lord's Supper, lawful vows (membership, baptism, ordination, marriage, etc.) and fasting upon special occasions; man is not free to add elements of human innovation such as drama.
- Does this church discipline members who persist in living in disobedience to Jesus Christ, the King and Head of the church?

When you find a church that teaches the Word of God, try going to that church for at least four weeks before eliminating it as a possibility.

Finally, bathe the whole effort in concerted prayer before the throne of grace. The matter of choosing a home church is of considerable importance to your spiritual health and eternal happiness. Pray and seek

God's will in the matter. (Pribble 1996)

CONCLUSION

This study has demonstrated the various forms of church government, church doctrines, and various teachings of different churches. The motives related to these various forms and teachings were to allow those looking for a church, to view from the outside, what may be inside the various churches.

There may be many who have knowledge of what churches believe but can't recognize truth from the outside. In Washington DC, at Metro Station, on a cold January morning in 2007, a man with a violin played six Bach pieces for about 45 minutes. During that time, approximately 2,000 people went through the station, most of them on their way to work.

After about three minutes a middle-aged man noticed that there was a musician playing. He slowed his pace and stopped for a few seconds, and then he hurried on to meet his schedule. About 4 minutes later, the violinist received his first dollar. A woman threw money in the hat and, without stopping, continued to walk. At 6 minutes a young man leaned against the wall to listen, then looked at his watch and started to walk again. 10 minutes later, a 3-year old boy stopped, but his mother tugged him along hurriedly. The boy stopped to look at the violinist again, but his mother pushed hard and the boy continued to walk, turning his head the whole time. 45 minutes went by and the musician played continuously. Only 6 people stopped and listened for a short while. About 20 gave money, but continued to walk at their normal pace. The man collected a total of $32.

After one hour he finished playing and silence took over. No one noticed and no one applauded. There was no recognition at all. No one knew this, but the violinist was Joshua Bell, one of the greatest musicians in the world. He played one of the most intricate pieces ever written, with a violin worth 3.5 million dollars. Two days before, Joshua Bell sold out a theater in Boston where the seats averaged $100 each to sit and listen to him play the same music.

This is a true story. Joshua Bell, playing incognito in the D.C. Metro Station, was organized by the Washington Post as part of a social experiment about perception, taste, and people's priorities.

The experiment raised several questions:
- In a common-place environment, at an inappropriate hour, do we receive beauty?
- If so, do we appreciate it?
- Do we recognize talent in an unexpected context?

An important conclusion that this experiment can bring, may be relevant to the choosing of a church.

What we can see in the lives of members of the church under consideration should be a reflection of what is in the inside. If we can just stop and see the beauty of real Christianity, it is not necessarily in the building but the sum of Christian living and worship of the heart.

A recent comic strip of "Dagwood" shows Alexander on the sofa with Dagwood.

Alexander: "I saw an awesome movie at the mall last night."

Dagwood: "Which one did you see?"

Alexander: "I don't remember the title, but the sound effects were so intense the walls actually shook"

Dagwood: "What was it all about?"

Alexander: "Boy, dad, you really miss the whole point of going to a multiplex theater, don't you?"

What is the real reason for worship? Is it the sound effects or sound doctrine?

May our great and gracious Lord, grant us all repentance from worldliness and give us the will to reform our worship practices, so that they are pleasing and acceptable to Him.

Give us the desire to choose a church whose purpose is to be one in Christ and glorify Him only.

BIBLIOGRAPHY

Bahnsen, Greg. *No Other Standard.* Tyler: Institute for Christian Economies, 1991.

Baker, Paul. *Contemporary Christian Music: Where it Came From, What it Is, Where is it Going.* Westchester: Crossway Books, 1985.

Barrick, Audrey. "Most Church Switchers Choose Non-TraditionalWorship." *The Christian Post,* April 5, 2007.

Crout, Robert E. *"What Kind of Church Do We Want."* Greenville SC: Robert E. Crout, September 23, 2006.

Crout, Robert E., *What Kind of Church Do You Want, Doctoral Dissertation* (Doctor of Theology, Newburgh Theological Seminary), Newburg, IN: Newburgh Press, 2012

Dingess, Ed. *Reformed Reasons.* July 25, 2011. http://reformed reasons (accessed Feb. 25, 2012).

Erickson, Millard J. Christian *Theology, 2nd ed.* Grand Rapids: Baker Publishing Group, 1998.

Gray, Steve. *What Kind of God do you want?* March 8, 2011. http://www.worldrevivalchurch.com (accessed Feb. 25, 2012).

Kosteberger, Andreas J. "Church Government" In *Encyclopedia of Christian Civilization,* n.d. http://onlinelibrary.wiley.com/doi/10.1002/9780470670606.wbecc0305/pdf

Kuiper, R. B. *For Whom Did Christ Die?* Grand Rapids: Eerdmans, 1959.

Kwasniewski, Peter. "Contemporary Music in Church." *Nova et Vetera* (International Theological Institute), 2005: 1-14.

Ladd, George Eldon. *Theology of the New Testament 2nd ed.* Grand Rapids: Wm. B. Eerdmans, 1993.

Lang, David Mashall. *The Arminian Apostolic Church.* 1973. www.wiekiepedia.org. The Arminian Church (accessed March 21, 2012).

Lewis, C. S. *Mere Christianity.* Grand Rapids: Harper e Collins, 1972.

Luther, Martin. "Address to the Christian Nobility of the German Nation." *Readings in European History,* 1906.

Morris, Dr. Henry M. *The Defender's Study Bible.* Grand Rapids: World Bible Publishers, 1995.

Motyer, J. Alex, Interview by *The Presbyterian Layman*, Robert

P. Mills. Retired principal of Trinity College, Bristol England (May 9, 2000).

Mumford, Bob. *The Truth About Baptism.* Raleigh: Lifechangers, 1975.

Patton, Francis Landey, Fundamental Christianity. [place: publisher]. 1926.

Pearlman, Myer. *Knowing the Doctrines of the Bible.* Springfield: Gospel Publishing House, 1937.

Peters, Pastor. *Pastoral Meanderings.* January 20, 2012. http://pastoralmeanderings.blogspot.com (accessed February 25, 2012).

"Presbyterian and Independency." *British Reformed Journal*, Number 11. 1995. July-August.

Preus, Rolf. Christforus. October 14, 2000. www.christforus.org (accessed March 28, 2012).

R. Scott, and H.G. Liddell. "Greek-English Lexicon." n.d.: 206. Schaeffer, Francis A. Doctrine. March 3, 2012. http://www.churchleadership.org/pages.asp? (accessed March 3, 2012). Schaff, Philip. What All Christians Believe. Grand Rapids: Baker, 2009.

Smith, James. Preach it Newsletter. March 22, 2012. preachit.org (accessed March 23, 2012).

Sun, Eryn. "Churches Called to Lay Down Youth Culture Idolatry in Worship." *Anglicans Ablaze,* March 2, 2012: 1-2.

Swatos, William H. *Episcopal Polity.* Sept 4, 2006. http://.wikipedia.org (accessed March 19, 2012).

Townes, Elmer. *What Faith is All About,* Wheaton, Illinois: Tyndale House Publishers, 1983.

Wardell, Isaac. Quoted by Bonnie McMaken in, "What's the Point of Worship." *Relevant Magazine,* Issue 51: May/June 2011 (May 23, 2011). Quoted by Erin Sun, g.v.

Wesley, John. "On Working Out Our Own Salvation," *The Works of John Wesley*. Kansas City: Beacon Hill, 1979.

APPENDIX I

CHICAGO STATEMENT ON BIBLICAL INERRANCY

PREFACE

The authority of Scripture is a key issue for the Christian church in this and every age. Those who profess faith in Jesus Christ as Lord and Savior are called to show the reality of their discipleship by humbly and faithfully obeying God's written Word. To stray from Scripture in faith or conduct is disloyalty to our Master. Recognition of the total truth and trustworthiness of Holy Scripture is essential to a full grasp and adequate confession of its authority.

The following Statement affirms this inerrancy of Scripture afresh, making clear our understanding of it and warning against its denial. We are persuaded that to deny it is to set aside the witness of Jesus Christ and of the Holy Spirit and to refuse that submission to the claims of God's own Word which marks true Christian faith. We see it as our three-day consultation in Chicago. Those who have signed the Summary Statement and timely duty to make this affirmation in the face of current lapses from the truth of inerrancy among our fellow Christians and misunderstanding of this doctrine in the world at large.

This Statement consists of three parts: a Summary Statement, Articles of Affirmation and Denial, and an accompanying Exposition. It has been prepared in the course of a the Articles wish to affirm their own conviction as to the inerrancy of Scripture and to encourage and challenge one another and all Christians to growing appreciation and understanding of this doctrine. We acknowledge the limitations of a document prepared in a brief, intensive conference and do not propose that this Statement be given creedal weight. Yet we rejoice in the deepening of our own convictions through our discussions together, and we pray that the Statement we have signed may be used to the glory of our God toward a new reformation of the church in its faith, life and mission.

We offer this Statement in a spirit, not of contention, but of humility and love, which we purpose by God's grace to maintain in any future dialogue arising out of what we have said. We gladly acknowledge that many who deny the inerrancy of Scripture do not display the consequences of this denial in the rest of their belief and behavior, and we are conscious that we who confess this doctrine often deny it in life by failing to bring our thoughts and deeds, our traditions and habits, into true subjection to the divine Word.

We invite response to this statement from any who see reason to amend its affirmations about Scripture by the light of Scripture itself, under whose infallible authority we stand as we speak. We claim no personal infallibility for the witness we bear, and for any help which enables us to strengthen this testimony to God's Word we shall be grateful.

SHORT STATEMENT

1. God, who is himself truth and speaks truth only, has inspired Holy Scripture in order thereby to reveal himself to lost mankind through Jesus Christ as Creator and Lord, Redeemer and Judge. Holy Scripture is God's witness to himself.
2. Holy Scripture, being God's own Word, written by men prepared and superintended by his Sprit, is of infallible divine authority in all matters upon which it touches: it is believed, as God's instruction, in all that it affirms; obeyed, as God's command, in all that it requires; embraced, as God's pledge, in all that it promises.
3. The Holy Spirit, Scripture's divine author, both authenticates it to us by his inward witness and opens our minds to understand its meaning.
4. Being wholly and verbally God-given, Scripture is without error or fault in all its teaching, no less in

what it states about God's acts in creation, about the events of world history, and about its own literary origins under God, then in its witness to God's saving grace in individual lives.

5. The authority of Scripture is inescapably impaired if this total divine inerrancy is in any way limited or disregarded, or made relative to a view of truth contrary to the Bible's own; and such lapses bring serious loss to both the individual and the church.

ARTICLES OF AFFIRMATION AND DENIAL

Article I.

We affirm that the Holy Scriptures are to be received as the authoritative Word of God.

We deny that the Scriptures receive their authority from the church, tradition, or any other human source.

Article II.

We affirm that the Scriptures are the supreme written norm by which God binds the conscience, and that the authority of the church is subordinate to that of Scripture:

We deny that church creeds, councils, or declarations have authority greater than or equal to the authority of the Bible.

Article III.

We affirm that the written Word in its entirety is

revelation given by God.

We deny that the Bible is merely a witness to revelation, or only becomes revelation in encounter, or depends on the responses of men for its validity.

Article IV.

We affirm that God who made mankind in his image has used language as a means of revelation.

We deny that human language is so limited by our creatureliness that it is rendered inadequate as a vehicle for divine revelation. We further deny that the corruption of human culture and language through sin has thwarted God's work of inspiration.

Article V.

We affirm that God's revelation within the Holy Scriptures was progressive.

We deny that later revelation, which may fulfill earlier revelation, ever corrects or contradicts it. We further deny that any normative revelation has been given since the completion of the New Testament writings.

Article VI.

We affirm that the whole of Scripture and all its parts, down to the very words of the original, were given by divine inspiration.

We deny that the inspiration of Scripture can rightly be affirmed of the whole without the parts, or of some parts but not the whole.

Article VII.

We affirm that inspiration was the work in which God by his Spirit, through human writers, gave us his Word. The origin of Scripture is divine. The mode of divine inspiration remains largely a mystery to us.

We deny that inspiration can be reduced to human insight, or to heightened states of consciousness of any kind.

Article VIII.

We affirm that God in his work of inspiration utilized the distinctive personalities and literary styles of the writers whom he had chosen and prepared.

We deny that God, in causing these writers to use the very words that he chose, overrode their personalities.

Article IX.

We affirm that inspiration, though not conferring omniscience, guaranteed true and trustworthy utterance on all matters of which the Biblical authors were moved to speak and write.

We deny that the finitude or fallenness of these writers, by necessity or otherwise, introduced distortion or falsehood into God's Word.

Article X.

We affirm that inspiration, strictly speaking, applies only to the autographic text of Scripture, which in the providence of God can be ascertained from available manuscripts with great accuracy. We further affirm that copies and translations of Scripture are the Word of God to the extent that they faithfully represent the original.

We deny that any essential element of the Christian faith is affected by the absence of the autographs. We further deny that this absence renders the assertion of biblical inerrancy invalid or irrelevant.

Article XI.

We affirm that Scripture, having been given by divine inspiration, is infallible, so that, far from misleading us, it is true and reliable in all the matters it addresses.

We deny that it is possible for the Bible to be at the same time infallible and errant in its assertions. Infallibility and inerrancy may be distinguished, but not separated.

Article XII.

We affirm that Scripture in its entirety is inerrant, being free from all falsehood, fraud, or deceit.

We deny that Biblical infallibility and inerrancy are limited to spiritual, religious, or redemptive themes, exclusive of assertions in the fields of history and science. We further deny that scientific hypotheses about earth history may properly be used to overturn the teaching of Scripture on creation and the flood.

Article XIII.

We affirm the propriety of using inerrancy as a theological term with reference to the complete truthfulness of Scripture.

We deny that it is proper to evaluate Scripture according to standards of truth and error that are alien to its usage or purpose. We further deny that inerrancy is negated by biblical phenomena such as a lack of modern technical precision, irregularities of grammar or spelling, observational descriptions of nature, the reporting of falsehoods, the use of hyperbole and round numbers, the topical arrangement of material, variant selections of material in parallel accounts, or the use of free citations.

Article XIV.

We affirm the unity and internal consistency of Scripture.

We deny that alleged errors and discrepancies that have not yet been resolved vitiate the truth claims of the Bible.

Article XV.

We affirm that the doctrine of inerrancy is grounded in the teaching of the Bible about inspiration.

We deny that Jesus' teaching about Scripture may be dismissed by appeals to accommodation or to any natural limitation of his humanity.

Article XVI.

We affirm that the doctrine of inerrancy has been integral to the Church's faith throughout its history.

We deny that inerrancy is a doctrine invented by scholastic Protestantism, or is a reactionary position postulated in response to negative higher criticism.

Article XVII.

We affirm that the Holy Spirit bears witness to the Scriptures assuring believers of the truthfulness of God's written Word.

We deny that this witness of the Holy Spirit operates in isolation from or against Scripture.

Article XVIII.

We affirm that the text of Scripture is to be interpreted by grammatico-historical exegesis, taking account of its literary forms and devices, and that Scripture is to interpret Scripture.

We deny the legitimacy of any treatment of the text or quest for sources lying behind it that leads to relativizing, dehistoricizing, or discounting its teaching, or rejecting its claims to authorship.

Article XIX.

We affirm that a confession of the full authority, infallibility, and inerrancy of Scripture is vital to a sound understanding of the whole of the Christian faith. We further affirm that such confession should lead to increasing conformity to the image of Christ.

We deny that such confession is necessary for salvation. However, we further deny that inerrancy can be rejected without grave consequences, both to the individual and to the church.

APPENDIX II

THE CHICAGO STATEMENTS ON BIBLICAL HERMENEUTICS

PREFACE

Summit I of the International Council on Biblical Inerrancy took place in Chicago on October 26-28, 1978 for the purpose of affirming afresh the doctrine on inerrancy of Scripture, making clear the understanding if it and warning against its denial. In the years that have passed since Summit I, God has blessed that effort in ways surpassing most anticipations. A gratifying flow of helpful literature on the doctrine of inerrancy as well as a growing commitment to its value give cause to pour forth praise to our great God.

The work of Summit I had hardly been completed when it became evident that there was yet another major task to be tackled. While we recognize that belief in the inerrancy of Scripture is basic to maintaining its authority, the values of that commitment are only real as one's understanding of the meaning of Scripture. Thus, the need for Summit II. For two years plans were laid and papers were written on themes relating to hermeneutical principles and practices. The culmination of this effort has been a meeting in Chicago on November 10-13, 1982 at which we, the undersigned, have participated.

In similar fashion to the Chicago Statement of 1978, we herewith present these affirmations and denials as an expression of the results of our labors to clarify hermeneutical issues and principles. We do not claim completeness or systematic treatment of the entire subject, but these affirmations and denials represent a consensus of the approximately one hundred participants and observers gathered at this conference. It has been a broadening experience to engage in dialogue, and it is our prayer that God will use the product of our diligent efforts to enable us and others to more correctly handle the word of truth (2 Tim. 2:15).

ARTICLES OF AFFIRMATION AND DENIAL

Article I.

We affirm that the normative authority of Holy Scripture is the authority of God himself, and is attested by Jesus Christ, the Lord of the Church.

We deny the legitimacy of separating the authority of Christ from the authority of Scripture, or of opposing the one to the other.

Article II.

We affirm that as Christ is God and Man in one person, so Scripture is, indivisibly, God's Word in human language.

We deny that the humble, human form of Scripture entails errancy any more than the humanity of Christ, even in his humiliation, entails sin.

Article III.

We affirm that the person and work of Jesus Christ are the central focus of the entire Bible.

We deny that any method of interpretation which rejects or obscures the Christ-centeredness of Scripture is correct.

Article IV.

We affirm that the Holy Spirit who inspired Scripture acts through it today to work faith in its message.

We deny that the Holy Spirit ever teaches to any one anything which is contrary to the teaching of Scripture.

Article V.

We affirm that the Holy Spirit enables believers to appropriate and apply Scripture to their lives.

We deny that the natural man is able to discern spiritually the biblical message apart from the Holy Spirit.

Article VI.

We affirm that the Bible expresses God's truth in propositional statements, and we declare that biblical truth is both objective and absolute. We further affirm that a statement is true if it represents matters as they actually are, but is an error if it misrepresents the facts.

We deny that, while Scripture is able to make us wise unto salvation, biblical truth should be defined in terms of this function. We further deny that error should be defined as that which willfully deceives.

Article VII.

We affirm that the meaning expressed in each biblical text is single, definite, and fixed.

We deny that the recognition of this single meaning eliminates the variety of its application.

Article VIII.

We affirm that the Bible contains teachings and mandates which apply to all cultural and situational contexts and other mandates which the Bible itself shows apply only to particular situations.

We deny that the distinction between the universal and particular mandates of Scripture can be determined by cultural and situational factors. We further deny that universal mandates may ever be treated as culturally or situationally relative.

Article IX.

We affirm that the term hermeneutics, which historically signified the rules of exegesis, may properly be extended to cover all that is involved in the process of perceiving what the biblical revelation means and how it bears on our lives.

We deny that the message of Scripture derives from, or is dictated by, the interpreter's understanding. Thus we deny that the "horizons" of the biblical writer and the interpreter may rightly "fuse" in such a way that what the text communicates to the interpreter is not ultimately controlled by the expressed meaning of the Scripture.

Article X.

We affirm that Scripture communicates God's truth to us verbally through a wide variety of literary forms.

We deny that any of the limits of human language render Scripture inadequate to convey God's message.

Article XI.

We affirm that translations of the text of Scripture can communicate knowledge of God across all temporal and cultural boundaries.

We deny that the meaning of biblical texts is so tied to the culture out of which they came that understanding of the same meaning in other cultures is impossible.

Article XII.

We affirm that in the task of translating the Bible and teaching it in the context of each culture, only those functional equivalents which are faithful to the content of biblical teaching should be employed.

We deny the legitimacy of methods which either are insensitive to the demands of cross-cultural communication or distort biblical meaning in the process.

Article XIII.

We affirm that awareness of the literary categories, formal and stylistic, of the various parts of Scripture is essential for proper exegesis, and hence we value genre criticism as one of the many disciplines of biblical study.

We deny that generic categories which negate historicity may rightly be imposed on biblical narratives which present themselves as factual.

Article XIV.

We affirm that the biblical record of events, discourses and sayings, though presented in a variety of appropriate literary forms, corresponds to historical fact.

We deny that any event, discourse, or saying reported in Scripture was invented by the biblical writers or by the traditions they incorporated.

Article XV.

We affirm the necessity of interpreting the Bible according to its literal, or normal, sense. The literal sense is the grammatical-historical sense, that is, the meaning which the writer expressed. Interpretation according to the literal sense will take account of all figures of speech and literary forms found in the text.

We deny the legitimacy of any approach to Scripture that attributes to its meaning which the literal sense does not support.

Article XVI.

We affirm that legitimate critical techniques should be used in determining the canonical text and its meaning.

We deny the legitimacy of allowing any method of biblical criticism to question the truth or integrity of the writer's expressed meaning, or of any other scriptural teaching.

Article XVII.

We affirm the unity, harmony, and consistency of Scripture and declare that it is its own best interpreter.

We deny that Scripture may be interpreted in such a way as to suggest that one passage corrects or militates against another.

We deny that later writers of Scripture misinterpreted earlier passages of Scripture when quoting from or referring to them.

Article XVIII.

We affirm that the Bible's own interpretation of itself is always correct, never deviating from, but rather elucidating, the single meaning of the inspired text. The single meaning of a prophet's words includes, but is not restricted to, the understanding of those words by the prophet and necessarily involves the intention of God evidenced in the fulfillment of those words.

We deny that the writers of Scripture always understood the full implications of their own words.

Article XIX.

We affirm that any pre understandings which the interpreter brings to Scripture should be in harmony with scriptural teaching and subject to correction by it.

We deny that Scripture should be required to fit alien preunderstandings inconsistent with itself, such as naturalism, evolutionism, scientism, secular humanism, and relativism.

Article XX.

We affirm that since God is the author of all truth, all truths, biblical and extra biblical, are consistent and cohere, and that the Bible speaks truth when it touches on matters pertaining to nature, history, or anything else. We further affirm that in some cases extra biblical data have value for clarifying what Scripture teaches, and for prompting correction of faulty interpretations.

We deny that extra biblical views ever disprove the teaching of Scripture or hold priority over it.

Article XXI.

We affirm the harmony of special with general revelation and therefore of biblical teaching with the facts of nature.

We deny that any genuine scientific facts are inconsistent with the true meaning of any passage of Scripture.

Article XXII.

We affirm that Genesis 1-11 is factual, as is the rest of the book.

We deny that the teachings of Genesis 1-11 are mythical and that scientific hypotheses about earth history or the origin of humanity may be invoked to overthrow what Scripture teaches about creation.

Article XXIII.

We affirm the clarity of Scripture and specifically of its message about salvation from sin.

We deny that all passages of Scripture are equally clear or have equal bearing on the message of redemption.

Article XXIV.

We affirm that a person is not dependent for understanding of Scripture on the expertise of biblical scholars.

We deny that a person should ignore the fruits of the technical study of Scripture by biblical scholars.

Article XXV.

We affirm that the only type of preaching which sufficiently conveys the divine revelation and its proper application to life is that which faithfully expounds the text of Scripture as the Word of God.

We deny that the preacher has any message from God apart from the text of Scripture.

www.ingramcontent.com/pod-product-compliance
Lightning Source LLC
Chambersburg PA
CBHW051805040426
42446CB00007B/530